T0094792

Tactics Time

1001 CHESS TACTICS
from the Games of Everyday Chess Players

By Tim Brennan and Anthea Carson
http://tacticstime.com

Version 1.69
Last Updated June 6, 2013

Colofon

© 2013 New In Chess
Published by New In Chess, Alkmaar, The Netherlands
www.newinchess.com
Originally published as a kindle edition.

All rights reserved. No part of this book may be reproduced, stored in a retrieval system or transmitted in any form or by any means, electronic, mechanical, photocopying, recording or otherwise, without the prior written permission from the publisher.

Cover design: LSDDesign
Supervisor: Peter Boel
Production: Rik Weidema

Have you found any errors in this book?
Please send your remarks to editors@newinchess.com. We will collect all relevant corrections on the Errata page of our website www.newinchess.com and implement them in a possible next edition.

ISBN: 978-90-5691-438-7

Dedication

This book is dedicated to YOU, the chess player seeking improvement in your game, wanting to win more games, and take your rating to the next level!

About the Authors

Tim Brennan is the creator of Tactics Time, which started off as a column in the quarterly Colorado Chess Informant Magazine. Tactics Time has grown into a blog, free e-mail newsletter, a Kindle eBook, and now a book! The focus has always been on real tactics from real player games, which Tim believes are the most instructive and useful types of tactics to study.
http://twitter.com/tacticstime
http://facebook.com/tacticstime
Tim@tacticstime.com

Anthea Carson is an active USCF tournament chess player, author, blogger, chess teacher, and mom. She is co-author of the children's chess book 'How to Play Chess like an Animal', and various thrillers, such as 'The Dark Lake'.
http://twitter.com/chessanimal
https://www.facebook.com/AntheaJaneCarson
nth_carson@yahoo.com

Contents

Preface

When Tim Brennan asked me to help him pick the best puzzles from his collection of thousands and thousands of tactics problems from real games I didn't realize how much I was going to gain from the experience. Tim was the editor of the Colorado Informant for several years, and has written the column called 'Tactics Time' for even longer. I noticed how his rating soared after his time editing those tactics articles, and now I can see why. It's not just doing puzzles. This is better, because the games are real. This makes a huge difference.

Everyone knows that the way to improve at chess is to do tactics puzzles, or if they don't know, they should. Tactics are the essence of chess. I have memorized openings, spending hours learning variation after variation only to miss a simple two move tactic late in the game. How frustrating is that?

I've also looked at my share of tactics books. Most tactics books have skewers and forks and discovery attacks and after a while you become familiar with the patterns. These are helpful books.

What I like about the tactics puzzles in Tactics Time is that the tactics you encounter are messy, don't look comfortable, aren't always visually pleasing. The typical tactics book has puzzles with nice, neat, tidy solutions but these are almost never what tactics look like in real games.

When you are used to looking at the puzzles in most books, you are expecting tactics to look a certain way. This can cause you to miss the ones that appear in real play. The tactics that show up in a game evolve out of the position. If you want to see the actual game that the tactic came from, which can be interesting too, those are also available in the database sold at http://www.tacticstime.com.

These puzzles come from games by average tournament or club players. In an average game, players make mistakes all the time. The mistakes can range from outright blunders to subtle positional errors that can be exploited if you know what you're looking for. A tactic is often there in a position where nothing looks wrong at all.

While I was looking through the puzzle collection to pick the best ones, I saw positions that looked like the ones I see when I play tournaments. Since I'm an average player, I am not typically playing GMs or even masters. You are less likely to encounter positions that leave open tactical opportunities in games with players of that strength, but the games of average players are like tactical goldmines. These puzzles will train you to look for tactics in games where you might otherwise have played your moves on autopilot.

I found myself seeing tactical moves I would not otherwise have seen after working on Tactics Time. I was amazed how many mistakes players at the 1500 to 1800 level make, and even many rated 1800 and above. Studying these puzzles is something I highly recommend. I would advise looking at them for 10 minutes a day for 30 days. Do that and see what the results are in your game.

Anthea Carson
October 2012

Introduction

Let me ask you a question...

Have you ever fumbled an important chess game? Be honest with me here. I want to know:

...have you ever been winning a game, only to blow it after you missed a simple two-move combination?

...have you ever spent hours, days or even months studying a chess book only to later realize that you didn't gain a single rating point from all that time and effort...and possibly even lost rating points?

...have you ever lost to a weaker opponent who you know you should've crushed?

...have you ever felt as if you can't improve at chess, and are 'stuck' in class player hell?

...have you ever felt that you should be better at chess, given how much time, energy and money you have spent on it?

...have you ever been beaten by a kid that only recently started playing? You might even have felt angry or humiliated because you have been playing for years, possibly before this kid was even born.

...have you ever missed an obvious move–or hung a piece for no reason–and just wanted to kick yourself afterward?

...have you ever had a chess loss keep you up at night?

...have you ever felt that your friends or opponents do not take you seriously as a chess player?

...have you ever missed 'simple' one- or two-move tactics in your games?

...have you spent dozens, possibly hundreds or thousands of hours studying chess, but still haven't reached your goals?

...have you ever felt like there has to be an easier way?

...have you ever felt that you're not playing up to your potential?

...have you ever had your rating stay basically the same for years, despite playing often?

...have you ever felt like just throwing in the towel and giving up because it seems like NOTHING will work...and that you should just accept it?

Sound familiar?

If you answered 'YES' to any of the above questions then I have some important news for you:

You are in the right place, and this is the right chess book for you.

Real Games from Real Players (Like You!)

This chess tactics book is different from any you have ever seen.

Why?

It is because all of the problems in it were taken from the games of real amateur chess players like you and me.

Many chess players have heard the often repeated idea that it is a good idea to study chess tactics if you want to improve, and that 'tactics are 99% of chess'.

This book is totally focused on improving your 'chess ability' – i.e. your ability to win games, and gain rating points. You will not learn any fancy new chess terms after going through this book, but you will develop strong habits of looking for the best move in each position, never overlooking the 'obvious', and always considering your opponent's threats, which will cause you to win more games, and raise your rating.

It is true that the fastest way to improve your chess rating is through the study and practice of tactics. However, there are major problems with the tactics puzzles that most chess books, software, magazines and websites contain today. Tactics Time will address these problems in a unique way.

The biggest problem of all is that they are not real!

Most of them contain way too many Queen sacrifices, smothered mates, and all kinds of 'cool moves'.

In the real world

- Positions are messy.
- Pawn structures are screwed up.
- Material is uneven.
- The openings are dubious.
- Pieces are hanging at the end of variations.
- Not everything works out perfectly.

Sure, smothered mates and Queen sacrifices are good to know, and a lot of fun to solve. You get a nice 'Ah Ha!' feeling after you solve one. They just don't translate into real world victories for you.

If you have limited time and energy to devote to chess, you want to study the types of positions that are happening all the time! Pins, forks, overloaded pieces, double attacks, back rank mates, loose and under-defended pieces.

Let me tell you a brief story...

In 2004 I became editor of the Colorado Chess Informant, the official state magazine for the Colorado Chess Association. I decided I wanted to have a tactics column in there, and started a column called 'Tactics Time', which continues to this day. This quarterly column later grew into a chess blog, award winning e-mail newsletter, and now this Book that you are reading.

When I started my tactics column, I wanted it to include games and positions from players in Colorado. I pictured having a column full of the same types of problems that I had been working on in Fred Reinfeld's classic 1001 tactics books. So I started collecting score sheets, entering games by hand into the computer, and looking at them closely.

What I found was shocking!

Most of these games, even by 'good' players, were being won by very primitive means. Players would play well for 20-30 moves, then 'fall asleep at the wheel', and then miss a simple one or two move combination.

Many of these blunders were so bad, I couldn't really even call them 'tactics', and they were too easy for me to publish in the column. There was rarely anything even close to the beautiful tactics in Reinfeld's books.

As I started looking at more and more games, I saw this happening ALL the time. But nobody was talking about it!

Chess players were talking in between rounds about how they were reading and studying 'How to Reassess Your Chess', and were then losing their next game to a simple Knight fork.

Articles in Chess Life never mentioned these things happening. NM Dan Heisman in his Novice Nook column on chesscafe.com was the only person I ever saw even mention these types of things. It was like the dirty secret of the chess world.

I started to collect more and more games. I became like a chess archeologist, digging in the waste baskets to collect barely legible score sheets filled with hieroglyphics in algebraic notation.

Sometimes people would send me a game to publish in the magazine, but this would only be their most brilliant victories. Nobody ever sent in a game where they lost to a two-move tactic that they missed, and their opponent saw.

Eventually, I took some time off from chess, and then came back to it a few years later.

After my return to the chess world, what I found was depressing. Most players had made absolutely no improvement, and despite spending hundreds of hours playing and possibly studying, were still missing these same 1-2 move tactics, and their rating had not gone up at all.

While I may sound like I am being hard on these players for not improving, in reality it is not their fault. The truth is that even if you do study a lot of the existing chess books out there, they are not going to help as much as they should.

How Tactics Time 1001 Real Problems from Real Games is Different

This book takes 'the good, the bad, and the ugly' positions of amateur chess, and puts them out there 'warts and all'.

I have to warn you that many of the problems in this book are not the types of chess problems that you may be used to solving. Some will be simple for you, and some you will get wrong, and you will think to yourself 'How did I miss such an easy problem?' This can be very annoying and frustrating.

The main point of this book is to get you in the habit of looking for the best move on every turn, to get good at doing an analysis of what is going on in a position, and to present lots of positions from real games so that you build your pattern recognition.

If you have formed bad habits solving the traditional chess tactics that are out there that can turn you into a Queen sacrificing machine, this book will help you fix those.

None of these problems are designed to be 'tricky', or fool you, or be clever. They are all real. Just find the best move in each position – that's it.

You aren't going to see problems where the solution is to underpromote a pawn to a Bishop, because moves like this happen one in a million games.

Why No Tactics from Grandmaster Games?

A common piece of advice given to aspiring chess players is to look at the tactics and positions from Grandmaster games. While this is not horrible advice, the types of positions that occur in Grandmaster games versus amateur games is like comparing the 100-meter dash at the Olympics to a bunch of third graders playing 'tag' at recess!

I believe that if you want to get good at playing against class players, the best way to do this is to look at the types of tactics and mistakes that are happening in their games, and learn from them, and apply them in your own games.

This book contains all sorts of interesting positions that you will never see at the Grandmaster level, but happen all the time in the 'trenches' of class player games. 'Miniatures' that lasted less than 20 moves, crazy unsound gambits, attack formations such as the 'Fishing Pole', flagrant violations of positional ideas, cheap traps, oversights and swindles.

Final Comments

This book assumes that you already know the basics of chess (how the pieces move), terms such as 'pin', 'fork', 'skewer', and how to read algebraic notation. If you need a refresher, Wikipedia has a lot of free information on the game, http://en.wikipedia.org/wiki/Chess.

Problems are given from the point of view of the side to move. If it is Black to move, the board is shown from Black's perspective.

Each solution is given on a separate page following the problem. The Kindle previewer doesn't show this, but the page breaks will show up in your Kindle reader.

Also, be sure to sign up for the award winning Tactics Time Chess Improvement e-mail newsletter. It is free, and comes out about 3 times a week with a new chess problem for you to solve, a fun quote, chess improvement tips, and the complete game score. The main focus is on chess improvement and pattern recognition, and like this book it has tons of positions that are new and never seen before from real games. You can see newsletter samples, and sign up at http://tacticstime.com/newsletter. You can contact us there as well if you have any questions, comments or feedback.

Good luck and have fun with this book.

Happy Tactics!

Tim Brennan
Anthea Carson
October 2013

1001 Chess Tactics

From the real games of everyday players

(1) Black to move

(2) White to move

(3) Black to move

(4) Black to move

(5) White to move

(6) Black to move

(7) White to move

(8) White to move

(9) White to move

(10) Black to move

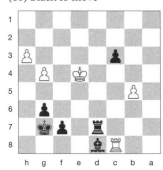

(11) White to move

(12) Black to move

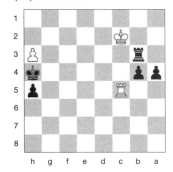

(13) White to move

(14) Black to move

(15) Black to move

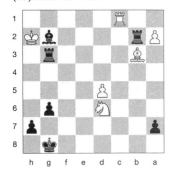

(16) White to move

(17) Black to move

(18) Black to move

12

(19) White to move

(20) Black to move

(21) White to move

(22) White to move

(23) Black to move

(24) White to move

(25) White to move

(26) White to move

(27) Black to move

(28) White to move

(29) Black to move

(30) White to move

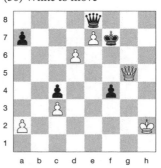

(31) Black to move

(32) Black to move

(33) Black to move

(34) Black to move

(35) White to move

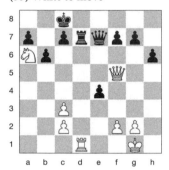

(36) Black to move

(37) Black to move

(38) White to move

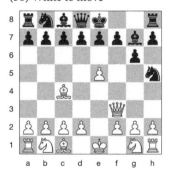

(39) White to move

(40) Black to move

(41) Black to move

(42) White to move

14

(43) White to move

(44) Black to move

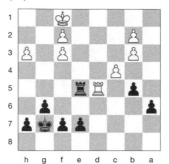

(45) Black to move

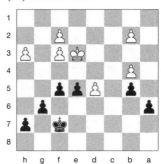

(46) White to move

(47) White to move

(48) Black to move

(49) Black to move

(50) Black to move

(51) White to move

(52) White to move

(53) White to move

(54) White to move

15

(55) Black to move

(56) White to move

(57) White to move

(58) Black to move

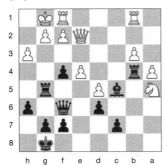

(59) Black to move

(60) White to move

(61) White to move

(62) Black to move

(63) Black to move

(64) White to move

(65) Black to move

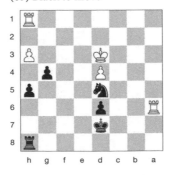

(66) Black to move

(67) Black to move

(68) White to move

(69) White to move

(70) Black to move

(71) Black to move

(72) White to move

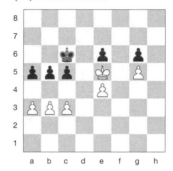

(73) Black to move

(74) White to move

(75) White to move

(76) Black to move

(77) White to move

(78) Black to move

(79) White to move

(80) Black to move

(81) Black to move

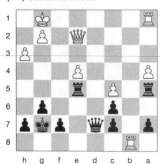

(82) White to move

(83) White to move

(84) White to move

(85) White to move

(86) White to move

(87) Black to move

(88) White to move

(89) White to move

(90) White to move

(91) Black to move

(92) White to move

(93) Black to move

(94) Black to move

(95) White to move

(96) White to move

(97) White to move

(98) Black to move

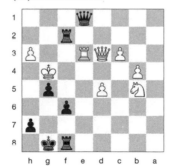

(99) Black to move

(100) Black to move

(101) Black to move

(102) Black to move

19

(103) White to move

(104) White to move

(105) White to move

(106) Black to move

(107) Black to move

(108) White to move

(109) Black to move

(110) White to move

(111) Black to move

(112) Black to move

(113) White to move

(114) Black to move

(115) White to move

(116) White to move

(117) White to move

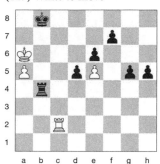

(118) White to move

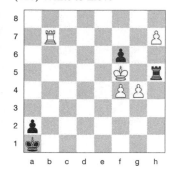

(119) White to move

(120) Black to move

(121) White to move

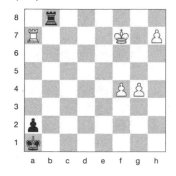

(122) Black to move

(123) Black to move

(124) White to move

(125) Black to move

(126) Black to move

(127) White to move

(128) Black to move

(129) White to move

(130) Black to move

(131) White to move

(132) White to move

(133) White to move

(134) Black to move

(135) White to move

(136) Black to move

(137) Black to move

(138) White to move

22

(139) Black to move

(140) Black to move

(141) White to move

(142) Black to move

(143) Black to move

(144) White to move

(145) Black to move

(146) Black to move

(147) Black to move

(148) White to move

(149) White to move

(150) White to move

23

(151) White to move

(152) White to move

(153) White to move

(154) White to move

(155) Black to move

(156) White to move

(157) White to move

(158) White to move

(159) White to move

(160) Black to move

(161) White to move

(162) White to move

(163) White to move

(164) White to move

(165) White to move

(166) Black to move

(167) Black to move

(168) White to move

(169) Black to move

(170) Black to move

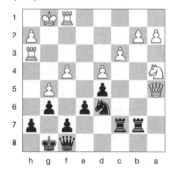

(171) White to move

(172) White to move

(173) White to move

(174) Black to move

25

(175) White to move

(176) White to move

(177) Black to move

(178) Black to move

(179) White to move

(180) White to move

(181) Black to move

(182) Black to move

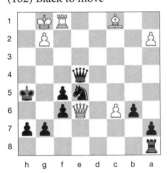

(183) Black to move

(184) White to move

(185) Black to move

(186) Black to move

(187) White to move

(188) White to move

(189) White to move

(190) Black to move

(191) Black to move

(192) White to move

(193) White to move

(194) White to move

(195) Black to move

(196) White to move

(197) White to move

(198) White to move

27

(199) White to move

(200) Black to move

(201) Black to move

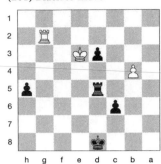

(202) Black to move

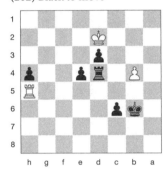

(203) White to move

(204) White to move

(205) Black to move

(206) Black to move

(207) Black to move

(208) White to move

(209) Black to move

(210) White to move

28

(211) White to move

(212) Black to move

(213) Black to move

(214) Black to move

(215) White to move

(216) White to move

(217) White to move

(218) Black to move

(219) Black to move

(220) White to move

(221) Black to move

(222) White to move

29

(223) White to move

(224) White to move

(225) Black to move

(226) White to move

(227) White to move

(228) Black to move

(229) White to move

(230) White to move

(231) White to move

(232) White to move

(233) Black to move

(234) Black to move

(235) White to move

(236) Black to move

(237) Black to move

(238) White to move

(239) Black to move

(240) Black to move

(241) White to move

(242) Black to move

(243) Black to move

(244) Black to move

(245) Black to move

(246) Black to move

31

(247) Black to move

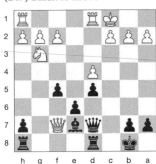

(248) Black to move

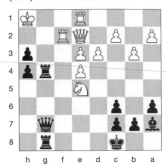

(249) Black to move

(250) White to move

(251) Black to move

(252) White to move

(253) White to move

(254) White to move

(255) White to move

(256) White to move

(257) White to move

(258) Black to move

(259) White to move

(260) Black to move

(261) White to move

(262) White to move

(263) Black to move

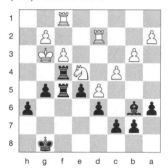

(264) Black to move

(265) White to move

(266) White to move

(267) Black to move

(268) White to move

(269) White to move

(270) Black to move

33

(271) White to move

(272) Black to move

(273) White to move

(274) Black to move

(275) White to move

(276) White to move

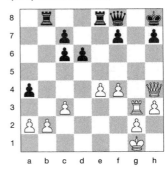

(277) White to move

(278) White to move

(279) White to move

(280) White to move

(281) Black to move

(282) White to move

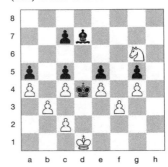

(283) Black to move

(284) White to move

(285) White to move

(286) Black to move

(287) White to move

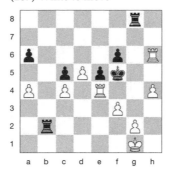

(288) Black to move

(289) Black to move

(290) Black to move

(291) White to move

(292) White to move

(293) White to move

(294) White to move

35

(295) Black to move

(296) Black to move

(297) Black to move

(298) Black to move

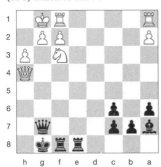

(299) Black to move

(300) Black to move

(301) Black to move

(302) Black to move

(303) Black to move

(304) Black to move

(305) Black to move

(306) White to move

(307) Black to move

(308) Black to move

(309) Black to move

(310) Black to move

(311) Black to move

(312) Black to move

(313) Black to move

(314) Black to move

(315) White to move

(316) White to move

(317) Black to move

(318) Black to move

37

(319) Black to move

(320) White to move

(321) Black to move

(322) Black to move

(323) Black to move

(324) Black to move

(325) Black to move

(326) White to move

(327) White to move

(328) Black to move

(329) Black to move

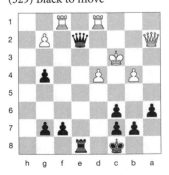

(330) Black to move

38

(331) White to move

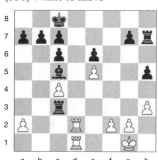

(332) White to move

(333) Black to move

(334) White to move

(335) White to move

(336) Black to move

(337) White to move

(338) Black to move

(339) White to move

(340) White to move

(341) White to move

(342) White to move

(343) Black to move

(344) White to move

(345) Black to move

(346) White to move

(347) Black to move

(348) Black to move

(349) White to move

(350) White to move

(351) White to move

(352) White to move

(353) Black to move

(354) Black to move

40

(355) White to move

(356) White to move

(357) White to move

(358) White to move

(359) White to move

(360) Black to move

(361) Black to move

(362) Black to move

(363) White to move

(364) White to move

(365) White to move

(366) White to move

41

(367) Black to move

(368) White to move

(369) Black to move

(370) White to move

(371) Black to move

(372) White to move

(373) White to move

(374) Black to move

(375) White to move

(376) Black to move

(377) White to move

(378) Black to move

(379) White to move

(380) Black to move

(381) Black to move

(382) Black to move

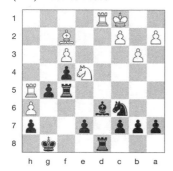

(383) White to move

(384) Black to move

(385) White to move

(386) Black to move

(387) Black to move

(388) Black to move

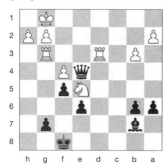

(389) White to move

(390) Black to move

43

(391) White to move

(392) White to move

(393) White to move

(394) Black to move

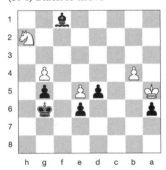

(395) Black to move

(396) Black to move

(397) Black to move

(398) White to move

(399) White to move

(400) White to move

(401) White to move

(402) White to move

44

(403) White to move

(404) Black to move

(405) Black to move

(406) White to move

(407) White to move

(408) White to move

(409) Black to move

(410) White to move

(411) Black to move

(412) White to move

(413) Black to move

(414) White to move

45

(415) White to move

(416) Black to move

(417) Black to move

(418) Black to move

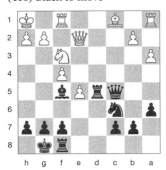

(419) Black to move

(420) White to move

(421) White to move

(422) White to move

(423) White to move

(424) Black to move

(425) Black to move

(426) Black to move

(427) White to move

(428) Black to move

(429) Black to move

(430) White to move

(431) White to move

(432) Black to move

(433) White to move

(434) White to move

(435) Black to move

(436) Black to move

(437) Black to move
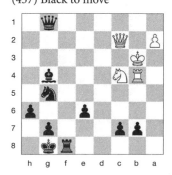

(438) Black to move

47

(439) Black to move

(440) Black to move

(441) White to move

(442) Black to move

(443) White to move

(444) Black to move

(445) Black to move

(446) White to move

(447) White to move

(448) Black to move

(449) Black to move

(450) Black to move

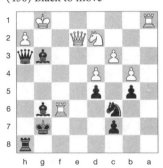

(451) White to move

(452) Black to move

(453) White to move

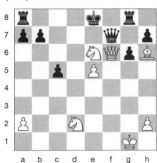

(454) Black to move

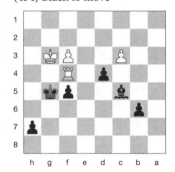

(455) Black to move

(456) Black to move

(457) White to move

(458) White to move

(459) Black to move

(460) White to move

(461) White to move

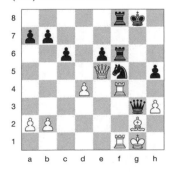

(462) White to move

49

(463) White to move

(464) White to move

(465) White to move

(466) White to move

(467) Black to move

(468) Black to move

(469) Black to move

(470) Black to move

(471) Black to move

(472) White to move

(473) White to move

(474) Black to move

(475) Black to move

(476) White to move

(477) Black to move

(478) White to move

(479) White to move

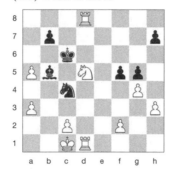

(480) Black to move

(481) White to move

(482) White to move

(483) White to move

(484) Black to move

(485) White to move

(486) Black to move

51

(487) White to move

(488) White to move

(489) White to move

(490) Black to move

(491) Black to move

(492) Black to move

(493) Black to move

(494) White to move

(495) Black to move

(496) Black to move

(497) Black to move

(498) Black to move

(499) Black to move

(500) Black to move

(501) Black to move

(502) Black to move

(503) White to move

(504) White to move

(505) Black to move

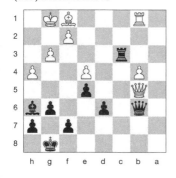

(506) White to move

(507) White to move

(508) Black to move

(509) Black to move

(510) Black to move

(511) White to move

(512) Black to move

(513) Black to move

(514) White to move

(515) White to move

(516) Black to move

(517) White to move

(518) Black to move

(519) Black to move

(520) White to move

(521) Black to move

(522) Black to move

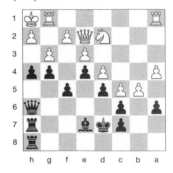

54

(523) White to move

(524) Black to move

(525) White to move

(526) White to move

(527) Black to move

(528) White to move

(529) White to move

(530) White to move

(531) White to move

(532) White to move

(533) Black to move

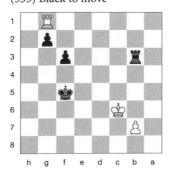

(534) Black to move

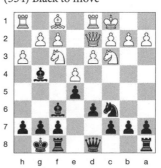

(535) White to move

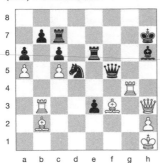

(536) White to move

(537) White to move

(538) Black to move

(539) White to move

(540) White to move

(541) Black to move

(542) Black to move

(543) White to move

(544) Black to move

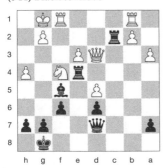

(545) Black to move

(546) Black to move

56

(547) White to move

(548) Black to move

(549) Black to move

(550) White to move

(551) Black to move

(552) White to move

(553) White to move

(554) White to move

(555) White to move

(556) Black to move

(557) White to move

(558) White to move

(559) White to move

(560) Black to move

(561) White to move

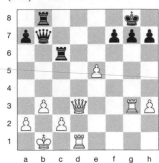

(562) White to move

(563) White to move

(564) Black to move

(565) Black to move

(566) White to move

(567) Black to move

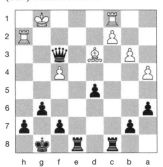

(568) Black to move

(569) White to move

(570) White to move

58

(571) Black to move

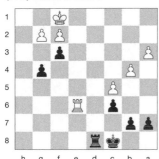

(572) White to move

(573) White to move

(574) White to move

(575) White to move

(576) Black to move

(577) Black to move

(578) Black to move

(579) White to move

(580) Black to move

(581) White to move

(582) Black to move

59

(583) Black to move

(584) White to move

(585) Black to move

(586) White to move

(587) Black to move

(588) Black to move

(589) White to move

(590) Black to move

(591) Black to move

(592) Black to move

(593) White to move

(594) Black to move

60

(595) White to move

(596) White to move

(597) Black to move

(598) Black to move

(599) Black to move

(600) Black to move

(601) Black to move

(602) White to move

(603) Black to move

(604) White to move

(605) Black to move

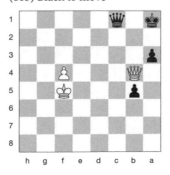

(606) Black to move

(607) White to move

(608) Black to move

(609) White to move

(610) White to move

(611) Black to move

(612) Black to move

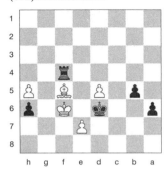

(613) White to move

(614) White to move

(615) Black to move

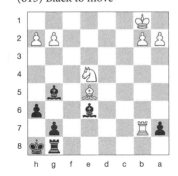

(616) White to move

(617) White to move

(618) White to move

62

(619) White to move

(620) Black to move

(621) White to move

(622) White to move

(623) Black to move

(624) Black to move

(625) White to move

(626) Black to move

(627) White to move

(628) White to move

(629) Black to move

(630) Black to move

63

(631) White to move

(632) White to move

(633) White to move

(634) White to move

(635) White to move

(636) White to move

(637) Black to move

(638) Black to move

(639) Black to move

(640) Black to move

(641) White to move

(642) White to move

(643) White to move

(644) White to move

(645) White to move

(646) White to move

(647) Black to move

(648) White to move

(649) White to move

(650) White to move

(651) Black to move

(652) Black to move

(653) Black to move

(654) White to move

65

(655) Black to move

(656) Black to move

(657) White to move

(658) Black to move

(659) White to move

(660) Black to move

(661) White to move

(662) White to move

(663) Black to move

(664) Black to move

(665) White to move

(666) White to move

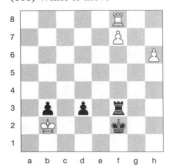

66

(667) White to move

(668) Black to move

(669) Black to move

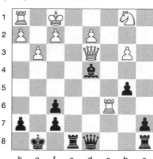

(670) White to move

(671) White to move

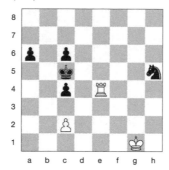

(672) White to move

(673) White to move

(674) White to move

(675) Black to move

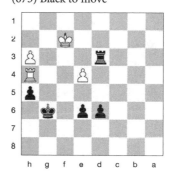

(676) White to move

(677) Black to move

(678) Black to move

(679) White to move

(680) White to move

(681) Black to move

(682) Black to move

(683) Black to move

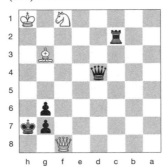

(684) Black to move

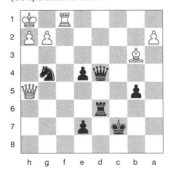

(685) Black to move

(686) White to move

(687) White to move

(688) White to move

(689) White to move

(690) White to move

(691) White to move

(692) White to move

(693) White to move

(694) White to move

(695) White to move

(696) White to move

(697) White to move

(698) White to move

(699) Black to move

(700) Black to move

(701) White to move

(702) White to move

69

(703) Black to move

(704) Black to move

(705) White to move

(706) White to move

(707) White to move

(708) White to move

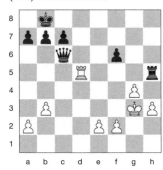

(709) White to move

(710) White to move

(711) Black to move

(712) Black to move

(713) Black to move

(714) Black to move

(715) Black to move

(716) White to move

(717) Black to move

(718) Black to move

(719) Black to move

(720) White to move

(721) Black to move

(722) White to move

(723) Black to move

(724) White to move

(725) White to move

(726) White to move

71

(727) Black to move

(728) White to move

(729) White to move

(730) White to move

(731) Black to move

(732) White to move

(733) White to move

(734) White to move

(735) Black to move

(736) White to move

(737) Black to move

(738) White to move

72

(739) Black to move

(740) Black to move

(741) White to move

(742) White to move

(743) Black to move

(744) Black to move

(745) Black to move

(746) Black to move

(747) Black to move

(748) Black to move

(749) Black to move

(750) Black to move

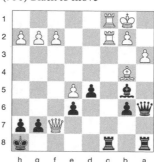

73

(751) White to move

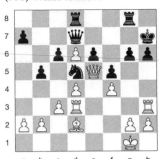

(752) Black to move

(753) White to move

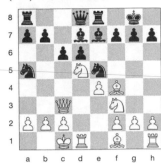

(754) White to move

(755) White to move

(756) Black to move

(757) White to move

(758) Black to move

(759) White to move

(760) White to move

(761) White to move

(762) White to move

(763) White to move

(764) White to move

(765) White to move

(766) Black to move

(767) White to move

(768) White to move

(769) White to move

(770) Black to move

(771) White to move

(772) Black to move

(773) White to move

(774) Black to move

75

(775) White to move

(776) Black to move

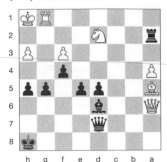

(777) Black to move

(778) Black to move

(779) Black to move

(780) White to move

(781) Black to move

(782) White to move

(783) White to move

(784) White to move

(785) Black to move

(786) Black to move

(787) Black to move

(788) White to move

(789) Black to move

(790) White to move

(791) White to move

(792) White to move

(793) Black to move

(794) White to move

(795) Black to move

(796) White to move

(797) White to move

(798) Black to move

77

(799) White to move

(800) White to move

(801) White to move

(802) Black to move

(803) Black to move

(804) Black to move

(805) White to move

(806) White to move

(807) White to move

(808) Black to move

(809) White to move

(810) White to move

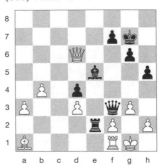

(811) Black to move

(812) White to move

(813) Black to move

(814) White to move

(815) White to move

(816) White to move

(817) White to move

(818) Black to move

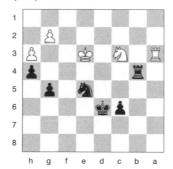

(819) White to move

(820) White to move

(821) White to move

(822) White to move

79

(823) White to move

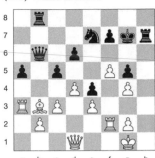

(824) Black to move

(825) Black to move

(826) White to move

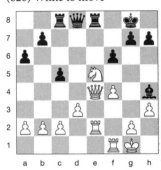

(827) White to move

(828) Black to move

(829) Black to move

(830) Black to move

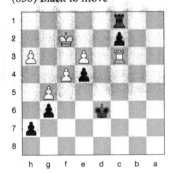

(831) Black to move

(832) White to move

(833) Black to move

(834) White to move

(835) White to move

(836) Black to move

(837) White to move

(838) White to move

(839) Black to move

(840) White to move

(841) Black to move

(842) White to move

(843) Black to move

(844) Black to move

(845) White to move

(846) Black to move

(847) White to move

(848) Black to move

(849) White to move

(850) White to move

(851) White to move

(852) Black to move

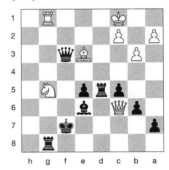

(853) Black to move

(854) Black to move

(855) Black to move

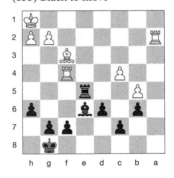

(856) White to move

(857) Black to move

(858) White to move

(859) White to move

(860) White to move

(861) White to move

(862) Black to move

(863) White to move

(864) White to move

(865) White to move

(866) White to move

(867) White to move

(868) Black to move

(869) White to move

(870) Black to move

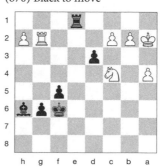

(871) White to move

(872) Black to move

(873) White to move

(874) White to move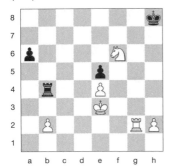

(875) White to move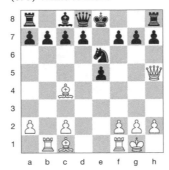

(876) Black to move

(877) Black to move

(878) White to move

(879) Black to move

(880) White to move

(881) Black to move

(882) White to move

84

(883) Black to move

(884) White to move

(885) White to move

(886) White to move

(887) Black to move

(888) Black to move

(889) Black to move

(890) Black to move

(891) Black to move

(892) Black to move

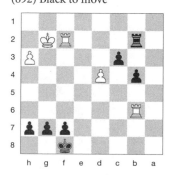

(893) Black to move

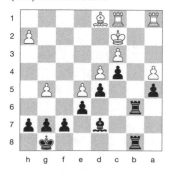

(894) White to move

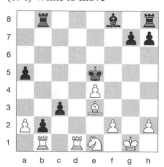

85

(895) White to move

(896) White to move

(897) Black to move

(898) White to move

(899) White to move

(900) White to move

(901) White to move

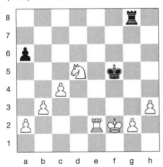

(902) Black to move

(903) Black to move

(904) Black to move

(905) Black to move

(906) Black to move

(907) Black to move

(908) Black to move

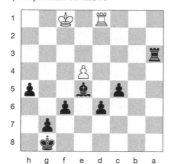

(909) White to move

(910) White to move

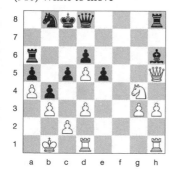

(911) Black to move

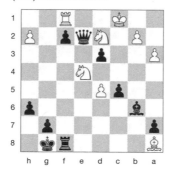

(912) White to move

(913) White to move

(914) Black to move

(915) Black to move

(916) White to move

(917) White to move

(918) White to move

87

(919) Black to move

(920) Black to move

(921) White to move

(922) White to move

(923) Black to move

(924) Black to move

(925) White to move

(926) Black to move

(927) White to move

(928) Black to move

(929) White to move

(930) White to move

(931) White to move

(932) White to move

(933) White to move

(934) White to move

(935) White to move

(936) Black to move

(937) Black to move

(938) White to move

(939) White to move

(940) White to move

(941) Black to move

(942) Black to move

89

(943) White to move

(944) White to move

(945) Black to move

(946) White to move

(947) Black to move

(948) White to move

(949) Black to move

(950) White to move

(951) Black to move

(952) Black to move

(953) White to move

(954) Black to move

(955) White to move

(956) White to move

(957) Black to move

(958) Black to move

(959) White to move

(960) Black to move

(961) Black to move

(962) Black to move

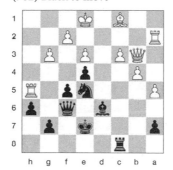

(963) Black to move

(964) Black to move

(965) Black to move

(966) Black to move

91

(967) Black to move

(968) Black to move

(969) Black to move

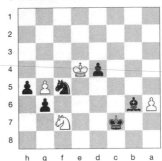

(970) Black to move

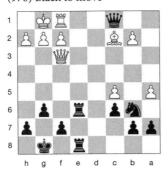

(971) Black to move

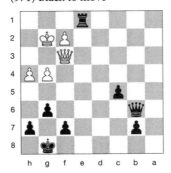

(972) Black to move

(973) Black to move

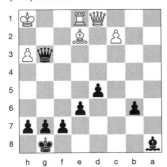

(974) Black to move

(975) White to move

(976) Black to move

(977) White to move

(978) White to move

92

(979) White to move

(980) Black to move

(981) Black to move

(982) White to move

(983) Black to move

(984) Black to move

(985) White to move

(986) Black to move

(987) Black to move

(988) White to move

(989) White to move

(990) White to move

93

(991) Black to move

(992) White to move

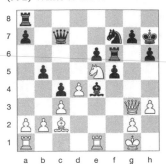

(993) White to move

(994) Black to move

(995) Black to move

(996) Black to move

(997) White to move

(998) Black to move

(999) Black to move

(1000) White to move

(1001) White to move

Solutions

(1)
10...Bb4+ unleashes the 'Atomic Bomb' of chess, the Double Discovered check. After either **11.Kf1** or **11.Kd1** Black mates with **11...Re1#**.

(2)
25.Nxd5 Rxd5 26.Qxd5 cxd5 27.Rxc7 Rxc7 28.Rxc7 wins a piece for White, taking advantage of the pinned c-pawn and the battery of Rooks on the c-file.

(3)
10...Nf3# is a smothered mate often seen in the trappy Blackburne Shilling Gambit variation of the Italian game.

(4)
13...Re8 pins the White Queen to the King.

(5)
27.Qe8+!! got a double exclam from Deep Rybka 4.1 and leads to checkmate after **27...Rxe8 28.Rxe8+ Kg7 29.Bf8+ Kg8 (or Kh8) 30.Bh6#.**

(6)
30...Rxc4 discovers an attack on the White Bishop on b6. After **31.bxc4 Bxb6 Black** has two Bishops for the Rook.

(7)
26.Qxd5 wins the under-defended pawn that was defended once, and attacked twice, and also attacks the undefended Rook on a8. If Black recaptures with **26...Qxd5** White forks the King and Rook with **27.Bxd5.**

(8)
25.Nd7 forks the two Rooks. If **25...Qxd7 26.Bxe5+** causes a lot of problems for Black, who has to give up his Queen to get out of check with either **26...Qg7** or **26...dxe5** (the d-pawn is now pinned to the Black Queen). White either wins the exchange (Rook for Knight), or more.

(9)
26.Nxe4 wins a pawn. If **26...Rxe4 27.Rxf8#.**

(10)
49...Bc7 blocks the attack from the Rook on c8 on the runaway c-pawn, and clears a path so that pawn 'could go all the way'. Black will Queen his pawn first after **50...c2** and **51...c1=Q.**

(11)
24.Rc3 puts the Queen between a rock and a hard place. The only safe square for the Queen is g5, but this allows for **25.Rg1** pinning and winning the Queen.

(12)
47...Rc3+ forces a trade of Rooks, leading Black to an easily won endgame.

(13)
19.Rxg6+ gets the Rook away from the f-pawn that is attacking it, and wins a pawn due to the fact that the f-pawn is pinned by the Bishop. The f-pawn being pinned to the Black King by White's light square Bishop is a pattern that comes up very frequently, and is a good one to memorize. 19.Rd6, forking the Queen and Bishop, is also a good move.

(14)
20...Nxg3!! takes a piece, while uncovering a discovered attack on the hanging White Queen on c2.
White took the bait, **21.Qxg6** and was mated with the beautiful **21...Nfe2#.** White has no way to save his Queen, and stop the mate threat.

(15)
36...Rh3+ leads to mate: **37.Kg1 Rh1#.**

(16)
52.Be5+ forks the King and Rook.

(17)
71...Nd3 was a winning move that was missed in the game. It attacks and will win the e5-pawn. If this pawn moves forward with e6, then Nc5+ forks the King and Pawn. If the pawn does nothing, Black just takes it. The e-pawn is won either way.

(18)
11...Bg4# is an interesting mate where both sides are using the idea 'The best defense is a good offense' to the extreme.

(19)
25.Qh6+ sets up a good mating pattern to know: *25...Kg8 26.Be6#.*

(20)
18...e4, which was missed in the game, blocks the Bishop's defense of the Knight on f5, and attacks it at the same time. White cannot save both, and will lose a piece.

(21)
16.Bf5 skewers the Black Queen and Rook.

(22)
41.Rd8+ sets up *41...Kh7 42.Qe4+* forking the King and Knight and if *42...Nf5 43.Rd5* forking the pinned Knight and the Queen. Black will lose the Knight.

(23)
41...Nd4+ forks the King and Queen. White blundered with 41.e4?? on the previous move allowing this fork.

(24)
10.Qc6+ deflects the Black Queen from her protection of the Rook on a8. *10...Qd7* is the only way to get out of check, but allows *11.Qxa8+* which wins the Rook.

(25)
13.Ne5+ unpins itself from the White Queen, and forks the King and Bishop.

(26)
17.Qg7# checkmating on Black's weak dark squares.

(27)
22...Nxe4 wins a pawn that is hanging, centralizes the Knight, which was hanging, and double attacks the Queen on f2 and pawn on c3. Nothing tricky about this one.

(28)
12.Bg5 pins the Knight to the Queen. Black cannot add a second defender to this piece.

(29)
11...Ne2# is an example of Anastasia's mate. This checkmate got its name from the novel *Anastasia und das Schachspiel* by Johann Jakob Wilhelm Heinse.

(30)
48.Qh5+ skewers the King and Queen. Black cannot get out of check and still protect the Queen.

(31)
13...Qh2# is a typical mating pattern in the Fishing Pole attack variation of the Ruy Lopez.

(32)
16...Na3# is a cute checkmate.

(33)
38...Ng3 threatens the Queen on e2 and a deadly 'hook mate' pattern with Rf1+. For example if White moves the Queen with *39.Qd3*, now Black has a mate with *39...Rf1+ 40.Kh2 Rh1#.*

(34)
17...Ng4 creates a discovered attack on the White Queen, which cannot move and still defend both the Bishop on e3 and the Knight on a4. If *18.e5,* blocking the attack from the bishop, *18...Nxe3 19.Qxe3 Rxa4* and Black is up a piece, taking advantage of the overloaded Queen.

(35)
Here Black found the surprising and creative *32.Nb8!!* adding a third attacker to the pinned Black Rook on d7 in an unusual manner. After *32...Kxb8 33.Rxd7* White has won a Rook for a Knight.

(36)
12...Rh1+ is a typical crazy position from the Fishing Pole attack. Black has given up a piece for the attack, and continues the 'sac, sac, mate' with *12...Rh1+ 13.Kxh1 Qh4+ 14.Kg1 g3 15.Nd6+ Kf8 16.Qh5 Qxh5 17.Re1 Qh2+ 18.Kf1 Qh1#.*
This variation is long, because White has some checks, and gives up his Queen to delay the mate, but the pattern is a good one to know.

(37)
16...Qh7 creates a battery that cannot be stopped, only delayed.

(38)
5.Qxf7# is a good old fashioned Scholar's Mate.

(39)
16.Bc5 attacks the Knight on b4 and sets up a discovered check with Nxc8 on the next move. Black cannot stop both threats at the same time.

(40)
Black infiltrates the dark squares with **22...Qf2+ 23.Kh1 Qh2#.**

(41)
28...Rc1+ leads to a simple back rank mate after **29.Rd1 Rxd1#.**

(42)
26.Bg5 pins and wins the Rook to the Queen.

(43)
29.Re8+ White has two attractive looking checks here, but **29.Re8+** is better. If **29...Rf8 30.Qe6+** followed by **31.Rxf8#.** If **29...Kf7 30.Qd7#.**

(44)
25...Rxd5 keeps it simple, and trades down into a winning endgame. Material is even, but White's pawns are such an isolated and doubled mess, that Black will have no trouble winning.

(45)
29...g5 makes it difficult for White to make any progress in this position, because of his doubled and isolated pawns.

(46)
18.Nxf7# is a nice smothered mate (and forks the King and Queen for extra style points).

(47)
13.Rxh7!! is a beautiful move that attacks the Rook on h8, and removes the defender of the g6-pawn. If **13...Rxh7 14.Qg6+** picks up a second pawn, forks the King and Rook, and forms a dangerous mating net around the Black King.

(48)
32...a5# is a cute mate with an assassin pawn.

(49)
36...d2 pushes the pawn and White will have no way to stop it from becoming a Queen.

(50)
17...c4 is a discovered attack, which attacks the Bishop on e3 and the Queen on b3 at the same time.

(51)
16.Nxe6 deflects the Queen away from defending the b7-pawn, which would allow White to win the Rook on a8. For example, **16.Nxe6 Qxe6 17.Bxb7 Nbc6 18.Bxa8.**

(52)
40.Rxg6!! got a double exclam from Fritz 12. White clears the way to protect his passed pawn on g7. If **40...Qxg6 41.Rg3** Black Queen moves, then White Queens a pawn with **42.g8=Q+.** This was a clever way for White to protect his passed pawn.

(53)
22.Rxe4+ sets up an absolute pin. After **22.Bxe4 23.Re1** White will win the Bishop with **24.f3.**

(54)
9.Qxc6+ forks the Knight and King and 'LPDO' - Loose Pieces Drop Off.

(55)
41...g5+ and mate after **42.Rxg5 fxg5#.**

(56)
9.Qf7+ and a pretty mate on the next move after **9...Qxf7 10.exf7.**

(57)
10.Nf6# The Knight smirks to the Queen and says 'I got this' and delivers smothered mate all by himself. The previous move, which was **9...Nbc6??,** was annotated by Fritz as 'strolling merrily down the path to disaster'.

(58)
25...f3 threatens the Queen on e2 and double attacks the vulnerable pawn on g2. If **26.Qxf3 Qxf3** and the g-pawn cannot recapture because it is pinned.

(59)
5...Bxb5 wins a piece. If **6.Nxb5 Qe5+** forks the Knight and King.

(60)
On the previous move Black played 10...Be6 to develop his bishop, stop the threat of Qxf7# and attack White's Queen. The move **11.Bxc6+** buys time for White, and wins a piece, removing the defender of the Bishop on b4, **11...bxc6 12.Qxb4**.

(61)
38.Qf4+ is a close range fork of King and Knight. White played 38.a5 instead, missing a chance to win a piece and simplify into a winning endgame.

(62)
7...Nxb5 After **8.Bxb5 Qa5+** wins a piece. This is a very valuable tactical pattern to know. Early Queen checks in the opening on the a- and h-files are great for picking up loose pieces on the 4th and 5th ranks. In the game Black played the first move of the combination with 7...Nxb5, but missed the kill shot Qa5+, and played the boring and passive a6?? instead. Remember to 'check all checks!'

(63)
32...Bg4 forks the two White Rooks.

(64)
15.Nd7+ is a nice discovery-double check that leads to mate after **15...Ka8** (only move) **16.Nb6+!! axb6** (only move) **17.Qa4#**.

(65)
36...Nb4+ forks King and Rook.

(66)
18...Qd6 threatens mate on h2 and the Knight on c5. White cannot defend both threats.

(67)
22...Qg4 puts the queen in position to infiltrate the light squares. No need for anything crazy here.

(68)
32.Re3 forks the Queen and Knight.

(69)
38.Qf4+ Black is in big trouble with his King stuck in the middle: **34.Qf4+ Be4 (1...Re4 2.Rd3#) (1...Kd5 2.c4+ Kc6 3.Rxe6+) 2.Rd3#**.

(70)
34...Nd3+ forks the King and Rook, and forces White to give up the exchange.

(71)
11...Nxf2 deflects the White King and forks the White Rook and Queen. If **12.Kxf2** then **12...d3+** discovers an attack on the King by the Bishop, winning back the sacrificed piece, and creating a mating net around the White King.

(72)
39.b4 prevents Black from doing the 'Every Russian Schoolboy knows' endgame trick with three pawns facing each other. If instead White plays **39.Kxe6** Black can get a passed pawn with **39...b4** (although White is still winning).

(73)
11...Ng4 threatens mate on h2 and discovers an attack on the Bishop on g5 at the same time.

(74)
27.Nh6# is a nice mate with Knight and Queen working well together.

(75)
38.Bxg7+ and mate after **38...Rxg7 39.Qxg7#**.

(76)
26...Rdxf2 grabs the f-pawn that was attacked 3 times and only defended once, and is threatening lots of dangerous double and discovered checks. Note that **29...Rfxf2** doesn't work, because the Rook on d2 is under attack, and Black has nothing after **29...Rfxf2 30.Rxd2 Rxd2+ 31.Kh1**.

(77)
11.Qh8+ Kf7 12.Ne5# is a nice mate with Knight and Queen working together like Batman and Robin. In the game White played 11. Qh8+ but then traded Queens, missing the mate in one.

(78)
15...Bf8 removes the defender of the Knight, which is also pinned to the Rook. Neither piece can move and defend the other.

(79)
55.Kg6 turns the King into an offensive weapon, forcing the Knight to move, and give up protection of the g5-pawn.

(80)
27...Rf7+ gets the Black King out of check, and also puts the White King in a discovered check at the same time, winning the White Queen on the next move. You did notice you were in check, right? ;-)

(81)
27...Qd4+ forks the White King and Rook on a1.

(82)
42.Qh8+ Rh7 43.Qxf6+ Kh5 44.Qg5#

(83)
15.Nh5 adds another attacker to the pinned Knight on f6, and clears the path for the Rook on g1 which indirectly pins the g7-pawn to the King.

(84)
10.Bxh6 picks up a pawn, while discovering an attack on the Black Queen. These types of tactics come up often when White castles Queenside.

(85)
40.Kd2 cuts off all the squares for the Black King. When the King has no squares, any check will be mate. Cutting off squares is often better than giving a check, and just chasing the King around. After Kd2 White is threatening Rd6#.

(86)
43.Nd3+ discovers an attack on Black's last remaining piece, the Knight on h5. When your opponent won't resign, little tactics like this can save you time and energy to help end the game quickly.

(87)
21...Rd8 causes Admiral Ackbar to exclaim 'It's a Trap!' The White Queen is trapped, with no safe squares.

(88)
White mates after **31.Qe8+ Rg8 32.Qxg8#**.

(89)
20.Nxd6 is a simple move that gets the Knight out of trouble (it was hanging on f5), wins a pawn that was under-defended, forks the Rook and Bishop, and offers a discovered attack from the Rook on the Queen if it moves on the next turn.

(90)
11.Nb5 attacks the Queen on c7, with a discovered attack on the Knight on e4. If **11...Qc6** to defend the Knight, **12.Qxe4 Qxe4 13.Nd6+** wins a piece.

(91)
17...Qb2 threatens the Rook on c1 and Knight on d2. White has no way to meet both threats.

(92)
25.Qc2 forks the Rook and Knight.

(93)
18...Qxc1+!! 'parts with the lady' as late Chess Life writer Jerry Hanken used to say: **19.Nxc1 Rd1#**.

(94)
8...c5 is the Noah's Ark trap. The Black Queen will have to move, and ...c4 will trap the light-square Bishop. This is a great trap to know!

(95)
9.Bxf7+! deflects the Black King from protection of the Black Queen. **9...Kxf7 10.Qxd8** and White is up a Queen for a Bishop. This type of tactic often comes up in the Sicilian Defense, when Black has a pawn on d6 and a Knight on f6, and White can play e5. If Black responds to e5 with dxe5, which looks normal, then this tactic can often be used.

(96)
24.Qxf4!! got a well deserved double exclam from Deep Rybka. If **24...exf4 25.Rxg7+** and White windmills like an NBA slam dunk contest winner: **25...Kh8 26.Rg5+** winning the Black Queen. White wins a piece.

(97)
14.Ng5 adds another attacker and creates an unstoppable mating net against the Black King. If **14...Ndf6 15.Qg8+ Nxg8 16.Nf7#** and against anything else White plays **15.Qxh7#**.

(98)
37...Rf4+ followed by **38.Kh5 Rh4#** (or **38...Qh4#**) ends the King Hunt.

(99)
21...Qxd3 is nothing fancy - it wins a piece that was under-defended. If **22.Nxe5** then **22...Qxc2 23.Rxc2 Rxe5**. If **22.Qxd3** then **22...Nxd3** forking the two White Rooks.

(100)
46...Ng5+ forks the King and Rook.

(101)
48...Ra1+ 49.Kd2 Rd3+ skewers the King and Rook on d1.

(102)
43...Rg2+ leads to mate. If *44.Kf1, Qe2#*. If *44.Kh1 Qe1+ 45.Rf1 Qxf1+ 46.Qg1 Qxg1#*.

(103)
12.Bh6 is a typical pinning technique when the White Queen and dark squared Bishop are attacking the King threatening *13.Qxg7#*. Black cannot take the Bishop, because the g-pawn is pinned. If he plays *12...g6*, then he loses the exchange after *13.Bxf8*. These types of moves can often seem to come out of nowhere, especially when the dark square Bishop moves from its home-square of c1.

(104)
30.Re1 skewers the Queen and the backward pawn on e6. If the Black Queen moves, for example, *30...Qd3 31.Rxe6+* and Black is in big trouble: *31...Kf8 32.Qxd7* and White is easily winning.

(105)
39.Rf7# is a midfield version of the 'hook mate' with all three minor pieces working nicely together.

(106)
22...Qg5# is another example of the Queen and Knight working nicely together to deliver mate. Sometimes longer range Queen checks are hard to see.

(107)
32...Bh3 adds a second attacker to the pinned Bishop on f1. White can defend against mate, but will have to give up his material advantage to do so.

(108)
12.Bc7 seals in the Black King, and prevents him from castling Queenside, and threatens *13.Qh5#* on the next move. Black is in a lot of trouble because of all of the weak squares around him.

(109)
16...Qf4+ double attacks the White King and the Bishop on c4, which is now attacked twice, and only defended once. Black wins a piece.

(110)
30.Bd6+ Ke8 31.Qg8+ skewers the King and Rook, winning a piece, or *31.Qc6+* forking the Rook and King.

(111)
7...Qxh3 takes a piece that is hanging. Keep it simple :-)

(112)
17...a6 removes the defender of the Bishop on d4, so Black can play *18...Qg4+* on the next move, forking the King and Bishop on d4.

(113)
13.Nd6+ has more forks than a Thanksgiving dinner.

(114)
50...f2 and Black wins the race to Queen his pawn. If *51.Rh1 Rg1+ 52.Rxg1 fxg1=Q+*. If *51.d7 f1=Q#*.

(115)
19.Nf6+ Not *19.Nc7+*, which is a more common forking-square, but in this case wins less material than forking the King and Queen. When you see a good move, look for a better one!

(116)
13.Qh5!! sets up a Blackburne mate pattern. If *13...gxh5 14.Bxh7#*. If *13...h6 14.Bxg6 Qxg5 15.Bxf7+ Kh7 16.Qxg5 hxg5 17.Bxe8* winning the Black Rook, which is what happened in the game.

(117)
41.Rb2!! forces a stalemate: the Black Rook is pinned, and White has no moves. This is my favorite tactics problem of all time, involving one of my best friends in a huge upset. That friend has a 'never resign' philosophy, and it paid off here.

(118)
59.Kg6 gets out of check, and forks the Rook and pawn. Not *59.gxh5??* which would be a stalemate.

(119)

14.Ne5 is a discovered attack on the Queen on h5 and adds a second attacker to the pinned Knight on d7. Black cannot meet both threats.

(120)

11...Nd3# This type of smothered mate is very common in the Budapest Gambit, and is known as the Kieninger Trap. This position actually came out of the Albin Counter Gambit, which has similar trappy lines in it.

(121)

62.Rxa2+ White simplifies into an easily winning endgame. Black will not be able to stop 3 passed pawns and an advanced King like White has.

(122)

10...Qxe4 forks the White Rook on h1 and Knight on d5. Rooks in the corners can be vulnerable to attacks by the Queen, when the fianchetto pawn is pushed, but the Bishop hasn't been developed yet.

(123)

28...Rxd3+ forks the King and Queen, and puts the Queen on the same file as the King for the follow up move **29.Qxd3 Nf2+** forking the White King and Queen.

(124)

28.Bc4 adds a second attacker to the backward e6-pawn. There is no way for Black to add a second defender, so the pawn will fall.

(125)

52...Qb2+ forks the King and Bishop on c2, winning a piece.

(126)

6...Qh4+ punishes White right out of the opening. After **7. g3** (the only way to get out of check) Black mates with either **7...Qxg3 8.hxg3 Bxg3#** or **7...Bxg3 8. hxg3 Qxg3#**. Be really careful when playing openings that include an early push of the f-pawn like The Bird, King's Gambit, Stonewall Attack, Dutch Defense, etc.

(127)

7.Qb3 creates multiple threats at the same time (the key to many successful tactics)- it attacks the weak b7-pawn, adds a second attacker to the knight on g8 threatening **8.Bxg8**, and threatens

8.Bf7+ Ke7 (...Kd7) 9.Qe6#. Black cannot meet all these threats at the same time.

(128)

12...Bxh3+ keeps it simple, and picks up a hanging piece with check, and will mate after **13.Kg1 Ne4+ 14.Be3 Qxe3#**.

(129)

16.Bb6 discovers an attack on the hanging Knight on e4. Black cannot save his Queen and the Knight both, so will lose material.

(130)

33...f5 is the first move of a two move combo. After the Knight moves, Black can play **34...e4** doing a discovered attack on the White Knight on f3 and the Rook on b2 at the same time. Such pawn wave attacks can be hard to see in advance.

(131)

19.Qxh7# is a common checkmate using the powerful battery of light square Bishop and Queen, with the White Knight helping cover the f7 escape-square.

(132)

16.Ne7+ and Black has to give up his Queen to avoid an Anastasia's mate. The game continued **16...Kh8 17.Qxh7+!! Kxh7 18.Rh3+ (18...Qh4 19.Rxh4#)**.

(133)

10.Bxh6 removes one of the defenders of the f7 pawn, and clears the way for the battery of Queen and Rook on the f-file. Black cannot replace this defender, and recapture at the same time, and is in big trouble.

(134)

23...Qb2 attacks both the Rook on c1 and the Bishop on e2. If **24.Re1 Nc3** adds two more attackers to the Bishop on e2, and White cannot meet all the threats.

(135)

14.Qh5+ and mate after **14...Kd7** (only move) **15.Qf7+ Qe7 16.Qxe7#**.

(136)

13...Nb6 is a discovered attack on both Bishops. White cannot save both.

(137)
22...Kg7 holds the fort, preventing moves such as Rf6, which would be devastating. Black is up a piece, but needs to survive first.

(138)
15.Nxf6+ checks the King, and discovers an attack on the h7-square. After either *15...Qxf6, 15...gxf6* or *15...Kh8* White plays *16.Qxh7#.*

(139)
11...Nxe5 takes a dangerous piece that is under-defended. Black has a couple of choices of what to do, but has to be careful. *11...Bxe2* looks logical, but then White has *12.Qxd7+.*

(140)
10...e5 is a pawn fork of Bishop and Knight.

(141)
9.Bxc6+ removes the defender of the Queen on d4 with check.

(142)
24...Qxa1 The Black Queen is trapped, so goes out with a bang taking two Rooks with her.

(143)
29...Nf4 is a clever move that helps cover escape-squares for the White King, and adds additional mate threats. White has two ways to capture this Knight, but both fail. If *30.gxf4 Qxf3* (the g-pawn is pinned). If *30.Qxf4 Qh1#.* Black is threatening to play *30...Qh2+ 31.Kf1 Qh1+ 32.Qxh1 Rxh1#.*

(144)
7.Bxf7+ discovers an attack on the hanging Black Queen on d4.

(145)
9...Qxd4+ forks the King and the White Bishop on c4. This type of forking tactic with the White King, White Bishop and Black Queen is common in class player games in the King's Gambit.

(146)
17...Qe4 leads to a forced mate. On the previous move, White played g3, which left horrible holes in his King's protection. White can only delay the mate with some spite checks: *18.Bxd6+ cxd6 19.Qxd6+ Bxd6 20.f3 Qe2 21.Rf2 Qxf2+ 22.Kh1 Qxh2#.*

(147)
10...Bxf2+ is a variation on Légal's Mate. *11.Ke2 Nd4#* This is a really good tactical pattern to know. Black actually played an unsound version of it, but got away with it.

(148)
19.Qxe6+ An easy mate in two with *19...Kf8 20.Qf7#.*

(149)
10.Qxb8+!! is a brilliant Queen sacrifice: *10...Nxb8 11.Nxc7#.*

(150)
32.Rxg7+ removes the defender of the Queen on f6: *32...Kxg7 (32...Bxg7) 33.Qxe6.*

(151)
35.Bxg7+ deflects the King from the f8-square: *35...Kxg7 36.f8=Q+* and mates soon after. In the game White grabbed a pawn with 35.Bxb6, and was still winning, but trading down and Queening the pawn is the much shorter route to victory.

(152)
25.Nxh7 If *25...Kxh7 26.Qxh5+* wins back the Knight with interest (the g6-pawn is now pinned to the Black King).

(153)
53.h7 pushes the pawn one step closer to becoming a Queen, giving up the less important Bishop as collateral damage.

(154)
27.a5 The wall of doubled pawns on the c-file, and the Black King being so far away, prevent Black from being able to stop the a-pawn from Queening.

(155)
37...Rg8 traps the White Queen.

(156)
41.Rxa8 deflects the Rook on e8 from the Queening-square: *41...Rxa8 42.Nf7+ Kg8 43.Nd8* and White will Queen his pawn.

(157)
40.Qf8# is a nice checkmate.

(158)
20.Bxf4 picks up a hanging piece.

(159)
34.Rxg6+ leads to a forced mate: *34...fxg6 35.Qxg6+ Kf8 36.Rf3+ Ke7 37.Rf7+ Kd8 38.Qf6+ Ke8 39.Qe7#.*

(160)
24...Nh4 threatens *25...Qxg2#*, and the family fork *25...Nf3+.*

(161)
11.Nd6+ Black was hoping to play a double discovered check with Nxc2+ but gets mated after *11...Kf8 12.Qxf7#.*

(162)
5.Bxh5# This USCF rated G/90 lasted only 5 moves: *1.d4 f5 2.e4 fxe4 3.Qh5+ g6 4.Be2 gxh5 5.Bxh5# 1-0.*

(163)
46.Rf6+ offers Black a Rook for a Knight so he can simplify into a winning endgame. If Black declines this offer, and plays *46...Kh5*, White picks up another pawn with *47.Rh6+*. If *46...Kg7 47.Rd6+* the discovered check wins the Knight.

(164)
32.Re7+ forks the King and Queen.

(165)
44.Qg8+ Kh6 45.Qh8#

(166)
29...Rg1 forces the Rook on f1 away from blocking the f-pawn.

(167)
18...Rg8 gets the Rook out of danger, and sets up a bone crushing discovered check on the next move.

(168)
53.Rd2+ forces Black to give up the defense of the Rook on c6 or trade Rooks, allowing White to easily Queen his a-pawn after *53...Rd6 54.Rxd6 Kxd6 55.a7.*

(169)
27...Nd6 The White Queen is forced away from her defense of the Knight on d7 after *28.Qa4 b5.*

(170)
30...Nc4 The White Queen gets trapped after *31.Qa6 Qe8* (or *...Qb8*) and *32.Ra7.*

(171)
9.Bf4 forces the awkwardly placed Queen to a bad square or into a lower value trade. After *9...Qe6 10.Nc7+* is a family fork.

(172)
23.Qxg7+ wins a piece and leads to mate after either
23...Kxe8 24.Qxg8+ Kd7 25.Qxf7+ Kd8 26.Bg5+ Qe7 27.Qxe7#
or: *23...Ke7 24.Bg5+ Kd7 25.Qxf7+ Ne7 26.Qxe7#.*

(173)
13.Nf6+!! got a double exclam from Fritz 13 and leads to mate after *13...Bxf6 (13...gxf6* or *13... Kh8) 14.Qh7#.*

(174)
16...Bh3+ leads to mate after *17. Kg1 Nxf3#.*

(175)
22.Bxe5 wins a piece because the d6-pawn is pinned. If *22...dxe5 23.Rxd8#.*

(176)
32.g3 traps the dark square Bishop who went after a poisoned pawn.

(177)
30...Nf4 traps the White Queen, who has no safe escape-squares.

(178)
19...g3 threatening *20...Qxh2#*. If *20.h3 Bxh3 21.gxh3 Qxh3* and White will have to give up material to avoid being mated.

(179)
6.Nfd5# is a fun checkmate from a Fischer Random (Chess 960) game.

(180)
21.Nxg7+ forces the Black King away from defending the f7 Rook from the White Queen.

(181)
13...Qh4+ leads to mate, exploiting the weak squares around the White King. *14.g3 Qxg3#*

Be careful with early f-pawn pushes in the opening, as they can leave you vulnerable to attacks like this.

(182)
34...Nf3+ Discovered attack, winning the Queen on e6.

(183)
18...Bxf6 wins a piece that is attacked 3 times, but only defended twice.

(184)
7.Bg5 puts the Black Queen in an awkward position – if the Queen moves, White has **8.Qd8#**.

(185)
29...Rxf5 wins a piece, as the e-pawn is pinned to the Queen.

(186)
15...Qxd2+!! 16.Kxd2 Nxe4+ discovers an attack on the White Queen on g7 from the Black Bishop on a1, and gets out of the mate threat on e7. This move would have turned things around for Black, who instead played **15...Qb5+** and was mated two moves later after **16.c4 Rg8 17.Qe7#**.

(187)
29.Rxd4 Qxd4 30.Rd2 skewers the Queen and the Knight on d6.

(188)
13.Nxe4!! If **13...Qxd4 14.Nf6+** (double check) **14...Kd8 15.Re8#**.

(189)
27.Qxe7+ would have been a brilliant Queen sacrifice leading to mate with the Boden's Mate pattern: **27...Kxe7 28.Bg5#**.

(190)
36...Qb7+ 37.Qg2 Rf2 38.Qxb7 Rh2# is a pretty Queen sacrifice and checkmate.

(191)
25...Qf5+ Black's Bishops are powerful and the White King has no defenders. **26.Ke1 Qf2#** or **26.Kg2 Qf2+ 27.Kh1 Qg1#**.

(192)
13.Nf6# is a neat checkmate taking advantage of the pinned g-pawn.

(193)
58.Rb4+ deflects the King away from the defense of the Bishop. **58...Kc5 59.Kxe3 Kxb4 60.f7 c2 61.f8=Q+** and White Queens first, with check. White can then play Qc8 and capture Black's pawn if it becomes a Queen.

(194)
62.g7 and Black cannot stop White from creating a Queen.

(195)
41...f2 – another runaway pawn that cannot be stopped.

(196)
35.Rg7 threatens mate with **36.Rh7#**. If **35...Rxg7 36.Qxg7#**. Black can put off mate with **35...Nf6** or **35...Ng5**, but these just delay the inevitable.

(197)
46.Rh8+ Kg6 (only move) **47.Nd6!** Attacks the Black Rook on b7 and threatens mate with **48.Bf5#**. Black cannot meet both of these threats, and will lose a piece.

(198)
27.Qf6 Sets up a mating net of **28.Qh6+ Kg8 29.Qh8#**. Black can throw in some checks, but can't stop mate.

(199)
17.Bf4+ ignoring the attack on the White Queen and giving mate after **17...Ne5 18.Bxe5 Qc7 19.Qxc7#**.

(200)
12...Qg6+ 13.Kh1 Qg2#.

(201)
83...d2 forces a trade of Rooks, leaving Black with an easily won endgame.

(202)
86...e3+ deflects the White King from his blockade of the d-pawn: **87.Kxe3 d2 88.Kxd4 d1=Q+** forks the King and Rook on h5.

(203)
32.Rxh4 Nothing tricky here. Just making sure you are paying attention :-) It looks like White might have a mating net, and can ignore the Queen, but there is no reason to do this.

(204)
27.Nd4+!! got a double exclam from Fritz 13 and leads to a forced mate: *27...Kg4 28.h3+ Kxh3 29.Nd1 Ng4 30.Re2 cxd4 31.Rh2+ Nxh2 32.Nf2#* or: *27...cxd4 28.Re5+ Kg4 29.Kg2 dxc3 30.h3#*

(205)
63...e1Q No need to get fancy and underpromote to a Knight.

(206)
51...d2+ was missed in the game: *52.Kxd2 Bxc1+*, removing the defender of the White Queen: *53.Kd1 Qxb3+.*

(207)
23...Rxa3 threatening *24...Ra1#* on the next move (the c2 Knight is pinned).

(208)
7.Nxf6# is a cute mate, punishing Black for his unusual Kingside pawn development.

(209)
23...Re1+ 24.Rxe1 Rxe1#

(210)
13.Qxg6 takes advantage of the f7-pawn being pinned. The Knight on g6 appeared to be defended by really wasn't. *13.Nxf7* is also good for White, but not as deadly as 13.Qxg6.

(211)
6.exf7# is an amusing checkmate.

(212)
27...Rxg2+ 28.Kxg2 Qg8+ forks King and Rook.

(213)
23...Rd1 creating a battery on the 8th rank, double attacking the Bishop on c1, threatening *24...Qf1#* and preventing the development of the g1-Knight.

(214)
26...Qxh1# A continuation of the previous problem, showing why the Knight on g1 was pinned.

(215)
18.Rxf7 wins a Rook. If *18...Nxf7 19.Qxf7+ Kh8 20.Qf8#* or *20.Qe8#.*

(216)
19.Bh6 builds a mating net. If *19...Rf7 20.Qe8+ Rf8 21.Qxf8#.*

(217)
30.Rdg1+ traps the Black King on the side of the board. After the Black King moves to the h-file, *31.Bf3+* with discovered check, and blocking the Black Bishop on d5: *31...Nh5 32.Rxh5#.*

(218)
19...c3 and White cannot stop *20...Qb2#.*

(219)
29...Qh6+ forks the King and the Bishop on h3.

(220)
32.Qg8# is a simple mate in one.

(221)
20...exd5 White got a little too fancy with in between moves. Both Queens are attacked, and so is the Knight on c5. After *20...exd5 21.Bxd8 Nb3* Black trades off the Queens, removes the attack on his Knight, forks the two Rooks, double attacks the Knight on c3, and still has an attack on the Bishop on d8.

(222)
7.Nd5 adds a third attacker to the pinned Knight on f6, which cannot be defended a third time.

(223)
14.Bg4 pins the Rook to the King.

(224)
48.Nxd5 wins a pawn and adds a second attacker to the Black Knight on c7. If *48...cxd5* (or *48...exd5*) *49.Bxc7 Bxc7 50.a8=Q+.* If *48...Na8,* blockading the a-pawn from Queening, *49.Nxe3* stopping Black's passed pawn.

(225)
13...Ba4 pins and adds a second attacker to the Knight on b3, which cannot be defended a second time.

(226)
14.Bxf5 exf5 15.Nxd5 wins a pawn, and forks the Bishop and Queen. The Black Queen has no squares to move to where it can still protect the Bishop on b4. White wins a piece with *16.Nxb4.*

(227)

23.Ng5+ exploits the pin on the f-pawn: **23...Kg8 24.Qxh7#.**

(228)

11...Nd5! adds a second attacker on the Knight on c3, and discovers an attack on the Knight on e5 from the Black Bishop on g7, winning a piece.

(229)

29.e7 is an unstoppable passed pawn.

(230)

48.Qd8 forks the Knight on b6 and the really bad Bishop on h8.

(231)

33.Bb3+ chases the King to the corner: **33...Kh8 34.Ng6+.** If **34...hxg6** White mates with **35.Rh3+ Bh4 36.Rxh4#** otherwise Black has to give up the Queen with **34...Qxg6 35.Rxg6.**

(232)

40.Rc1 with the threat Rc8, pinning the Queen to the King. **40.Nd5**, which was played in the game, is also good, but doesn't win as quickly.

(233)

29...Qe2 threatens mate on g2 and double attacks the Rook on f1 and the Knight on b2.

(234)

14...Ng4 creates a mating net against the White King.
Some sample lines, analysis by Fritz 13:
1. -+ (-#6): 15.Bxf7+ Kd8 16.Qxg4 hxg4 17.Bh5 Qxh5 18.f4 Qxc5+ 19.Rf2 g3 20.Nc3 Qxf2#
2. -+ (-#6): 15.Bxd6 cxd6 16.Bxf7+ Ke7 17.Qxg4 hxg4 18.Bh5 Rxh5 19.f4 g3 20.Nc3 Qh2#
3. -+ (-#4): 15.Qxg4 hxg4 16.f4 g3 17.Bxf7+ Kxf7 18.Nc3 Qh2#
4. -+ (-#2): 15.Rd1 Qh2+ 16.Kf1 Qh1#

(235)

24.Bxg7 removes the defender of the Knight on f6.

(236)

21...Bxf2+ breaks up the King's pawn defense, wins a pawn, deflects the King away from the defense of the Bishop on h2 and attacks the Rook on e1.

(237)

46...Bb8+ and mate after **47.Kh3 Rh2#.**

(238)

4.Qh5# is a variation on Fool's Mate.

(239)

17...Nf2# is a cute mate in a position where both sides are threatening mate in one.

(240)

13...Qg3+ 14.Kh1 Qxh3+ 15.Kg1 Nf3# A common checkmating theme in the Fishing Pole attack.

(241)

7.Qd5 and Black has no good way to defend the f7-pawn. The only reasonable response is **7...Nh6**, but after **8.Bxh6** Black is still in big trouble. A good trick to know in the Scotch Gambit.

(242)

17...Bxe4+ overloads the White Rook like a dishwasher on Thanksgiving: **18.Rxe4 Qf1#.**

(243)

14...Qh7 In the game White played 14...g4, but 14...Qh7 is much more efficient, and a common attack formation in the Fishing Pole opening. This move creates a battery on the h-file. White will have to give up major material to avoid being mated.

(244)

6...Bxf2+ This is a good opening trick to know in the Budapest Gambit. This type of tactic is common when White declines the gambit (for example 1.d4 Nf6 2.c4 e5 3.d5). White either gets mated or loses major material after **7.Kxf2 Ne4+ 8.Ke3 Qg5+ 9.Kd3 Nf2+** forking the King and Queen:
8.Ke1 Qh4+ 9.g3 Qxg3#
8.Kf3 Qh4 9.Ke3 Qf2+ 10.Kd3 Qd4+ 11.Kc2 Nd2+ 12.e4 Bxe4+ 13.Bd3 Qxd3#
If **7.Kd2 Ne4+ 8.Kc2 Bxg1** to set up the threat of **9...Nf2+** discovered check, winning the Queen.

(245)

16...Qf3 and Black cannot stop **...Ng4+** and **...h2#.**

(246)
11...Qg3, threatening **...Qh2#.** White can only delay mate with a series of giving up pieces and spite checks. This pattern is another good one to know in the Fishing Pole attack.

(247)
15...Bg5+ White grabbed a pawn on f7 with his Queen on his last move, but it was unsafe because of the discovered attack **15...Bg5+.** When you castle Queenside instead of Kingside, your King can be more vulnerable to these types of checks.

(248)
24...Rg1+ 25.Kh2 Qg3# and Black cashes in on the nice battery he created on the g-file.

(249)
16...Qd4+ forks the King and Rook.

(250)
14.Rd1 pins and wins!

(251)
20...Bg4+ removes the White King from defending the pinned White Rook, and brings another piece into the attack with tempo (a check). After the King moves to the d-file, Black plays gxf3. Playing gxf3 right away is OK too, but the Bishop check is a little more accurate.

(252)
14.Bg4 pins the Rook to the King.

(253)
14.Qc4+ and Black cannot stop the mate: **14...Nd5 15.Qxd5+ Bc6 16.Qxe6#.**

(254)
36.Qa6 threatening **37.Qb7#.** If **36...Kc7** to escape, **37.Qb7+** forks the King and Bishop on b6: **37...Kd6** (only move) **38.Qxb6.** White now gains back the material advantage and has three passed pawns on the Queenside that are becoming very powerful.

(255)
25.Ng6+ On the previous move Black played f6, attempting to kick the White Knight from its nice outpost, but missed this.

(256)
12.Bg5 pins and adds a second attacker to the Knight on f6. There is no way for Black to defend this piece a second time, and he will lose it.

(257)
25.exd6 cxd6 26.Nf6+ forks the King and Queen. This is better than 26.Rxe7+ forking the King and Queen, which was played in the game. This trades Rook and Knight for Queen, which is worse than winning the Queen for just the Knight.

(258)
10...Qxa5!! is a brilliant Queen sacrifice deflecting the White Queen from her protection of the c2-square, threatening **11.Nc2#.** There are no safe squares for the White Queen, and she will be lost or White will be checkmated.

(259)
26.Ne7+ Kh7 27.Qh5# with a variation on Anastasia's Mate with a Queen instead of a Rook.

(260)
36...Bd1+ 37.Ka3 Ra4# A forced mate missed in the game.

(261)
28.Nxd6+ forks the King and Queen. The c7-pawn is pinned.

(262)
14.Nxc5 threatens the Queen on d7 and removes the defender of the Knight on f2. Black got over-aggressive with **13...Nxf2** on the previous move, and will lose a piece.

(263)
38...Rxe4 39.fxe4 Rxe1 The f-pawn was pinned.

(264)
51...Nxb6 52.Kxb6 Rxa6+! Black gives up two pieces to stop White's passed pawns, and transposes into an easily won endgame.

(265)
12.Qf7#

(266)
27.Re6 threatens the Queen and the check capture on f6.

(267)
37...g2 There is no way for White to stop the dangerous passed pawns.

(268)
14.f6# Discovered Checkmate.

(269)
22.Nxh5 gxh5 23.Qxh5. White wins a Rook and pawn for a Knight. In the game, White retreated his knight with *22.Nf3?.*

(270)
25...Rxe2+ removing the defender of the White Rook on g1.

(271)
35.Rxc7+ forks the Black King and Bishop.

(272)
11...Ne2# not only wins the Queen but checkmates the King!

(273)
14.Qg3 gets the Queen out of danger, attacks the Knight and the g7-pawn, and still guards the Knight on c3. Quite a lot for one move! The move *14.Qe3?* is similar, but not as good. It gets the Queen out of danger, and prepares to trap the Black Queen with Rfb1 (or Rab1) and Rb3. This move looks good, but allows *14...Qxb4.*

(274)
10...Qg3 with the threat *Qh2#.* The f2-pawn is pinned from the Black Bishop on c5. A common mating theme in the Fishing Pole attack. If *1.hxg4 hxg4*, and now the Black Rook on h8 supports the mate on h2 or h1.

(275)
12.Re1 wins the Queen.

(276)
26.Qf6+ Qg7 is the only move to block the check and then *27.Qxg7#.*

(277)
47.Nb3+ forks the King and Rook. White missed this move, playing Ne6+, and went on to lose the game. Even stronger players miss simple one move Knight forks, especially in fast time controls and blitz.

(278)
31.Nxf7 and if the Black King captures the White Knight, he no longer guards his own Knight.

(279)
22.Qxb5+ axb5 23.Be3 wins a piece because the Bishop is attacked twice, can't be defended a second time, and if it moves, it exposes the Rook on a8.

(280)
12.Bxf7+ Qf7+ deflects the Black Queen away from the mate threat on g2. White can follow up with *13.Qxf7+ Kxf7* when Black has multiple pieces under attack and can't save them all: *14.dxe7 Bxe7 15.gxh3* and White is up a piece.

(281)
17...Nf3+ and after the pawn captures the Knight on f3, the Bishop recaptures. Mate in one is then unstoppable via Rh1.

(282)
45.Kd2 and mate next move via c3 is unstoppable.

(283)
12...Bd5 pins and wins the Knight. It is attacked twice (by the Knight on d6 and the Bishop on d5). If *13.Ref1* (or *13.Rae1*) adding a new defender, *13...f5* and the Knight can't move because of the pin on the Queen.

(284)
29.Qe8+! and mate to follow with either *29...Rf8 30.f7+ Kh8 31.Qe5#* or *29...Rxe8 30.Rxe8+ Rf8 31.Rxf8#.*

(285)
30.Rxf6 removes the defender of the h5-pawn. If *30...gxf6 31.Qh5+ Kg8 32.Qh6 Ne7 33.Qg7#.*

(286)
13...Qxf2+ removing the defender of the back rank leads to *14.Qxf2 Rxd1#.* or *14.Kh1 Qxc2* and Black is up a Queen.

(287)
32.g4+ forces Black to give up his Rook to get out of check with *32...Rxg4+ 33.Rxg4.*

(288)
14...Qh7 and White will have to give up a ton of material to avoid mate on the h-file.

(289)
16...Bxh3 and the pawn can't recapture because of the pin on the g-file from the Black Queen to the White King. This is a very common tactical pattern, and a good one to know.

(290)
18...Qg4 threatens mate in one. If White plays g3, Queen h3 seals the deal.

(291)
36.Rh7+ deflects the Black King, and creates a mating net:
36...Kxh7 37.Qxf7+ Kh8 38.Bxe5#
36...Kf8 (or 36...Kg8 or 36...Kf6) 37.Qxf7#

(292)
14.Qf6+ This stops the checkmate by forcing a Queen trade.

(293)
5.Bxf7+ A common opening trick that wins a pawn. If *5...Kxf7 6.Ng5+* and *7.Qxg4* winning back the sacrificed piece.

(294)
21.Rc3 not only threatens the Black Queen directly, it also threatens *22.Qb3+* starting a smothered mate by screening the Black Queen from the third rank. Black's best chance is to give up the queen for rook and knight by *21...Qxc3 22.bxc3 fxe5 23.Rxe5* but he will be down a queen for a rook (having sacrificed a piece on move 17). Black instead played *21...Qh6* and after *22.Qb3+* allowed the smothered mate: *22...Kh8 23.Nf7+ Kg8 24.Nxh6+ Kh8 25.Qg8+ Rxg8 26.Nf7#.*

(295)
39...Rxc5 wins a Pawn. The d4-pawn is pinned to the undefended Rook on d2.

(296)
26...Nf3+ forks the King and Queen taking advantage of the pinned g-pawn.

(297)
20...Rbh4 and White either gets mated, or a skewer of the King and Rook on a1 on the next move. For example *21.f3 (or 21.f4) 21.Rh1+ 22.Kf2 Rxa1*. If *21.g3 Rh1+ 22.Kg2 Be4+ 23.f3 R8h2#.*

(298)
23...Rxf3 The g-pawn is pinned, and can't recapture.

(299)
14...Qg3+ and mate next move: *15.Kh1 Qh2#*. The f-pawn is pinned by the Bishop on c5.

(300)
28...f5# is a cute checkmate, also forking the King and Rook.

(301)
10...Bh3 and White cannot stop mate via Bg2 and Rh1#.

(302)
14...Bg3 and White cannot stop *Qxh2#.*

(303)
14...Be6 forks the White Queen and White Knight. White's best option is to give up the Queen for two pieces, but he is still losing. For example, *15.Nxh8 Bxd5 16.Ng6 Qf6 17.exd5 Qxg6* and Black has a Queen for Rook and Knight. If *15.Qxe6 Qxe6 16.Nxh8 0-0-0* and the White Knight is trapped.

(304)
14...Rh1+ sacrifices the Rook for mate in two via Qh4+ and Qh2. This move doesn't allow White a chance to capture the pawn on g3. Who says that tripled pawns are bad? :-)

(305)
5...Bxf2+ is a common discovered attack trick in the Budapest Gambit: *6.Kxf2 Ng4+ 7.Ke1 Qg5.*

(306)
5.Nxg6 gets both pieces that are attacked out of trouble, and takes advantage of the h7-pawn being pinned to the Black Rook on h8. If *5...hxg6 6.Qxh8.*

(307)
15...Qxg3+ and mate on the next move, taking advantage of the pinned f-pawn: *16.Kh1 Qg2#.*

(308)
29...fxe4+ wins the Queen with a discovered check.

(309)
24...Rxg3# The pawn on f2 is pinned by the 'peek-a-boo' Bishop on a7.

(310)
36...Qxb3 wins the Knight. If the Rook recaptures, White gets checkmated via **37...Rd1#**.

(311)
11...Qh3 keeps the pressure on without losing the Queen. White cannot stop mate. For example **12.Rxf2 Nf3+ 13.Rh2 Qxh2#**.

(312)
15...Re1+ leads to mate after **16.Bf1 Ne2+**. The White Rook on f2 is pinned from the Black Bishop on c5, and the White Bishop on f1 is pinned by the Black Rook on e1: **17.Kh1 Nxf2+ 18.Kh2 Ng4+ 19.hxg4 hxg4+ 20.Bh6+ Rxh6#**, or **16.Rf1 Ne2+ 17.Kh1 Rxf1#**.

(313)
13...hxg4 clearing the h-file with the threat Qh2#. Mate cannot be stopped.

(314)
15...f3 with the threat **16...Qg2#** and mate cannot be stopped: **16.Qxf3 gxf3 17.Ne3 Qxh2+ 18.Kf1 Qh1#** or **16.Ne3 Qxh2+ 17.Kf1 Qh1#**

(315)
6.Nxe5 wins a pawn and threatens **7.Bf7#**, if **6...dxe5 7.Bf7+** overloads the Black King: **7...Kxf7 8.Qxd8** winning the Queen.

(316)
29.Rxc6 wins a pawn. If **29...Qxc6 Bxd5+** forking the Queen and King.

(317)
50...Rxb7+ Both Rooks are under attack. Black wins a dangerous passed pawn, and will get his Rook back on the next move with **51.Nxd3** transposing into an easily won endgame.

(318)
34...Bxe6 wins a pawn that appears to be protected. If **35.Rxe6 Nd3+ 36.Ke4 Rxe6+ 37.Kxd3** Black ends up an exchange ahead.

(319)
18...Qxg5# An interesting checkmate with almost the entire black army helping out.

(320)
35.Rxd7 wins a piece: **35...Kxd7 36.Nc5+** forking the King and Rook.

(321)
9...Qe3# and White is trapped by his own army.

(322)
17...Qh2+ 18.Kf1 Qh1#

(323)
18...Rxh3+ Black's pieces are surrounding the White King like a pack of rabid wolves: **19.gxh3, Qxh3#**.

(324)
16...hxg4 removing the defender of the White Bishop on h4, and opening the h-file for an attack on the White King.

(325)
23...h3 threatening **24...hxg2#**. White has some spite checks, (24. d7+ Kxe7 27. d8=Q+, etc), but cannot stop mate: **24.gxh3 Rxh3 25.Qxh3 Qxh3#**.

(326)
18.Bg5 adds a second attacker to the pinned Black Bishop on h4. If the Bishop moves, **18...Bxg5 19.Rxh7** winning the Queen for a Rook and Bishop.

(327)
10.Qd8# is a good mating pattern to know for quick kills in the opening.

(328)
26...Qxg2+ skewers the White King and Queen.

(329)
Just taking the Queen is fine, but **28...Re3+** leads to mate. For example **29.Rd3 Rxd3+ 30.Kc4 b5+ 31.Kc5 Rc3+ 32.Qc4 Rxc4#**.

(330)
22...Rxg3 wins the Bishop as the f-pawn is pinned.

(331)
27.Rd8# From the same game as above. Black found a nice tactic that won a piece, then missed a back rank mate 2 moves later.

(332)
15.Qh4 blocks the checkmate and saves the Queen.

(333)
19...Qh3+ 20.Kd2 Qd3#

(334)
6.Qe5+ forks the Black King and Rook.

(335)
7.Ng5 adds a second attacker to the f7-pawn, and discovers an attack on the loose Knight on h5.

(336)
26...Qf3#

(337)
16.e5 dxe5 17.Ne4 traps the awkwardly placed Black Queen. Black would have to play 16...Nxe5 to prevent the Queen getting trapped, but this gives up a piece for a pawn.

(338)
10...Qxd1 removes the defender of the f2-pawn. **11.Rxd1 Nxf2** wins a pawn, gets the Knight out of danger, attacks the Rook on d1, and sets up a discovered check for the next move.

(339)
12.Nxb4 Bxb4 13.Qa4+ forks the Black Bishop and King, winning a piece.

(340)
16.Qd5 attacks the Knight on c6, which is pinned to the Black Rook on a8. Black has no way to defend this Knight.

(341)
34.Qa5+ Kb7 35.Qb6#

(342)
35.Rb8+ and the Black King is forced to block the Rook file so the pawn can Queen. **35...Ka4 36.a7 Rb4 37.a8=Q.**

(343)
20...Bd6 skewers the White Queen and the Knight on h2. If the Queen moves, **21.Qd4** then **21...Bxh2+** wins a piece. If the White Knight recaptures on h2 with **22.Nxh2**, then **22...Qxg2#.**

(344)
11.Nxd6+ taking advantage of the pinned e-pawn. If **11...Qxd6 Bxd6**, and if **11...Kd7 12.Bb5+ Kc7 13.Nxf7+** forking the Queen and Rook with discovered check.

(345)
23...c5 The pawn on b4 is pinned to the White Knight on c4. Next move Black can win a pawn with **24...cxb4,** taking advantage of the a3-pawn pinned to the White Rook on a1.

(346)
14.Nxf7! takes a pawn, attacks the Queen on d8, and sets up a nasty discovered check if Black captures the Knight: **14...Kxf7 15.Bc7+ Kg8 16.Bxd8** winning the Black Queen.

(347)
41...Re2+ If **42.Kf1 Qf2#.** If **42.Kh3 Bc8** wins the Queen. If **42.Kh1** Black has a mating net with **42...Re1+ 43.Kg2 Qg1+ 44.Kh3 Qf1+ 45.Kg4 Rxe4+ 46.f4 Rxf4+ 47.gxf4 Qg2#.**

(348)
44...Ne5+ forks the King and Rook.

(349)
11.Bxh7+ leads to mate after **11...Kh8 12.Bg6+ Kg8 13.Qh7#.** Note that 11. Qxh7+ allows the Black King to escape, and doesn't lead to mate.

(350)
33.Bxe3 and if the pawn recaptures, then **34.Rf8+** wins the Bishop which has to block on e8.

(351)
52.Bf6+ chases away the Black King, and White will proceed with **53.d7+** and **54.d8=Q.**

(352)
18.Nxe7+ and if the Queen recaptures, **18...Qxe7,** it no longer guards the Bishop on c4, allowing **19.Qxc4+** winning a piece.

(353)
2...Qh4+ with a variation on Fool's Mate after *3.g3 Qxg3#*.

(354)
26...Qxf2+ 27.Kh1 Qf1+ 28.Rxf1 Rxf1# is a good back rank mate pattern to know.

(355)
10.Bd5 forks the Knight and Rook.

(356)
12.Ng1 traps the Queen after *12...Qf5* and *13.Bd3*.

(357)
17.Bxf7+ wins 2 pawns, *17...Kh8 18.Qxd7*.
If *17...Rxf7 18.Re8+ Rf8 19.Qd5+ Kh8 20.Rxf8#* with a good back rank mate pattern to know.

(358)
23.Qe8+ wins the Knight.

(359)
10.Nh4 traps the Black Queen.

(360)
14...Nxe3+ captures a pawn, forks the King and Queen with check, and discovers an attack on the White Knight on d2 from the Black Rook on d8. After *15.fxe3 Rxd2* Black gets his piece back, and ends up a pawn ahead.

(361)
10...Qxh2# A common mating pattern in scholastic games.

(362)
18...Qd3+ forces a Queen trade. White was threatening mate with Qxa7#.

(363)
22.Bd5+ and after the pawn blocks, the Bishop captures the pawn and it's mate: *22...c6 23.Bxc6#*.

(364)
32.Rd8+ and after the Black King moves to the only safe square e6, *32...Ke6* White gives check with the Knight: *33.Nc5+*.The King can only go to e7, *33...Ke7*. Then the Rook checks on d7, guarded by the Knight, and wins the Bishop: *34.Rd7+ Kf8 35.Rxb7*.

(365)
15.Ng7#

(366)
12.Nxd6+ winning a piece with discovered check.

(367)
14...Bxb3 Discovered attack, pinning the White Queen to the King.

(368)
17.Nc7+ and it will be mate next move since the King can't move to the d-file: *17...Kf8 18.Rd8#*.

(369)
11...g4 forks the Queen and Knight.

(370)
25.Qd4+ and it's mate next move after the Queen captures the Rook which blocks the check: *25...Rf6 26.Qxf6#*.

(371)
19...Bxf3 and the pawn can't recapture because it's pinned.

(372)
15.Bb5 pins the Black Knight on c6 to the Queen. There is no way to add another defender, and Black will lose a piece.

(373)
30.Be4+ forks the Black King and Rook.

(374)
15...e4 Double discovered attack on both Knights. White can't save them both.

(375)
19.c7 and Black cannot stop the pawn from queening.

(376)
16...Qxc3+ and Black will skewer the White King and Queen on the next move, with either *17.Kxf4 Qe5+* or *17.Ke2* (or *17.Kf2*) *17...Qc2+*.

(377)
19.Bc5 attacks the Black Rook on f8, to deflect it from defending the critical f7-square.

(378)
20...c3 An interference tactic, attacking the White Queen, and after **21.bxc3** the queen is blocked from the protection of the White Knight on a5, allowing **21...Qxa5** winning a piece.

(379)
29.Rh6#

(380)
30...Nd5# A pure checkmate.

(381)
14...Nxg4 15.fxg4 Qxg4+ (forking the King and Bishop) **16.Kh1 Qxg5** picks up two pawns.

(382)
22...Ba3+ deflects the White King: **23.Kb1 Rxd1#**.

(383)
18.Rxe5 safely takes the hanging Bishop on e5. There is no back rank mate for Black since the light squared Bishop can retreat to f1 to block.

(384)
26...Rh1+ skewers the White King and Rook: **27.Kf2 Rxd1 28.Kxg3** and Black is up the exchange.

(385)
24.Bxh6 The g-pawn is pinned, and cannot capture the White Bishop. Black has to play g6 and give up the exchange to avoid the devastating Rxg7+: **24...g6 25.Bxf8.**

(386)
32...Re1+ forking the White King and Rook. If **33.Rxe1 dxe1=Q.** If **33.Kh2 Rxb1.**

(387)
27...Rd4 pins the Bishop to the Queen and double attacks the Bishop. It can't be defended after **28...Re2 29.Rc2.**

(388)
27...Qe1# A good mating pattern to know.

(389)
39.Qh8+ Kg6 40.Qg7+ Kh5 41.g4+ forks the King and Queen.

(390)
15...Nfd5 attacks the Queen. **16.Qc4** The only safe square for the Queen. **16...b5** traps the Queen. White can save the Queen with **17.Bxh7+ Kxh7 18.Qe2 Nxa2** but loses a Bishop in the process.

(391)
22.Rxd7+ removes the guard of the Bishop on b7: **22...Kxd7 23.Qxb7+.** If the King moves to the 8th rank, Black also loses the Rook on a8: **23...Ke8 24.Qxa8+.** If the Black King moves forward **24.Re6+** leads to mate **24...Kc5 25.Qb5+ Kd4 26.c3#.**

(392)
21.Bc5+ skewers the King and Knight on e7, which is now double attacked. **21...Kc6 22.Nxe7+** wins a piece. Black must take **22...Qxe7 23.Bxe7** which wins Queen and also game later, otherwise if **22...Kb5?** there is a mate in 4: **22...Kb5 23.a4+ Ka6 24.b5+ Ka5 25.Bb4+ Kb6 26.Nd5#.**

(393)
28.Ba6# A Boden's Mate style checkmate.

(394)
42...Be2 traps the Black Knight.

(395)
13...Qb4+ wins the pesky Bishop on b7.

(396)
19...Qxe5+ Even though Black can capture the Bishop on f7, he should first capture the pawn on e5 with check, since he can still win the Bishop after White gets out of check with **20...Kxf7.**

(397)
26...Rg2+ 27.Kh1 Rxh3# is a nice mate in two.

(398)
23.Rxh7#

(399)
40.Qxe6 and even though White gives up the Queen, there is no way for Black to stop the d-pawn from queening: **40...Qxe6 41.d7 h6 32.d8=Q+.**

(400)
5.Bxa6 wins a piece after **5...Nxa6 6.Qa4+** forking the King and Knight.

(401)
19.Bh3 pins and adds a second attacker to the Black Knight on g4, pinning it to the Queen, if **19…f5 20.Rxf5** winning a pawn.

(402)
11.f5 traps the Bishop.

(403)
20.Nxf7#

(404)
17…Qg5 threatens mate with **18…Qxg2**, and sets up a deadly discovered check. For example **18.g3 Nxh3+ 19.Kg2 Qxd2** winning the White Queen.

(405)
39…Rf6# An interesting checkmate.

(406)
16.Ne4 forks the Black Queen and Bishop. There is no retreat-square for the Queen where she can still protect the Bishop.

(407)
8.Bxf7+ When the King moves up it is then checkmate from the Knight on d5: **8…Ke7 9.Nd5#** This is the famous Légal's Mate. White has cleverly sacrificed his Queen on d1 for this sneaky checkmate.

(408)
17.Qh6+ and after the King moves to either g8 or h8, the White Knight is traded for the Knight on f6, which then allows the Queen to capture the pawn on h7 with checkmate: **17…Kg8 18.Nxf6+ Qxf6 19.Qxh7#**.

(409)
13…Ne4 Discovered attack. The White Knight on c3 is double attacked and pinned, so Black will either win the Knight or capture the White Rook on a1 after the White Knight moves: **14.Nxe4 Bxa1**.

(410)
9.Nd6# Smothered mate.

(411)
17…Bc5 pins the White Queen to the King.

(412)
19.Nc8+ forces the Black King to the 8th rank, and after any King move, **20.Nxd6** (discovered check) **20…Ke7 21.Rxf7#**.

(413)
13…Nd4 and White cannot save the Queen and prevent the smothered mate Nc2#. If **14.Qe3 Nc2+** forks the King and Queen.

(414)
9.Nb5 threatening the Queen, and also mate with **10.Nc7#**. The Black Queen cannot find a safe square to guard c7, so this wins the Queen, since Black needs to stop the mate.

(415)
10.Nf6# Double Discovered Checkmate.

(416)
6…Nxe5 Unfortunately you can't take the Queen or you get Legal's mated via **7.Bxf7 Ke7 8.Nd5#**.

(417)
18…e4 attacks the White Bishop on d3 and discovers an attack on the White Knight on d6. Black wins a piece.

(418)
19…Bd3 skewers the White Queen and Rook.

(419)
20…Bxc3 and White has no good way to recapture. The b-pawn is pinned to the Rook.

(420)
13.Bg6+ Double discovered check. **13…Kd7 14.Be8**. A beautiful checkmate!

(421)
12.Qh5 attacks the Knight on g5, and threatens mate on f7. Black can't meet both threats, and will lose a piece.

(422)
15.Bf7+ Kf8 16.Qh6#

(423)
18.Ne5 attacks the Black Knight on d7, and discovers an attack on the Black Bishop on b7: If **18…Nxe5 Bxb7** and Black has both his Knight and Rook under attack. If **18…Bxg2 Nxd7** forking the Black Queen and Rook.

(424)
19…Nf5+ 20.Kg4 Rh4+ 21.Kg5 Qd8# (**21…Be7#**) and the Fat Lady has sung.

(425)
9…Bb3 10.Qd1 Nc2 forks the Queen and Rook.

(426)
20…Rxh3# The g-pawn is pinned.

(427)
32.Ra8+ All roads lead to mate:
32…Qxa8 33.Nf6+ Kh8 34.Qxh7#
32…Rd8 33.Rxd8+ Qe8 34.Rxe8#

(428)
4…g6 prevents the mate on f7. White is in trouble after **5.Qh4 Be7** and there is no way to save the Knight that is pinned and attacked twice. Black wins a piece.

(429)
14…Nc2+ removes the White King from the defense of the f2-pawn, which is now attacked twice: **15.Kh1 Rxf2.**

(430)
31.Rg7+ Kh8 32.Qh4 leads to mate.

(431)
14.Bxh7+ The classic 'Greek Gift' sacrifice. White will follow up the attack with moves like Rh3, Qh5, and Black is in trouble regardless if he accepts the 'gift' or not. This is a complicated tactical idea, but a good one for future study, as it comes up often.

(432)
52…Rf2+ Discovered check, helping Black trade down into an easily won endgame: **53.Kg3 Rxh2 54.Kxh2.**

(433)
17.Qg4+ leads to mate: **17…Kd6 18.Be7+ Kxe5 19.d4#** or **17…Qe6 18.Qxe6#.**

(434)
16.Ne7# A cool checkmate with 2 Knights.

(435)
7…Ba6+ runs White out of luck. Giving up a piece with **8.Nb5** is the only way to avoid the checkmate. If **8.Kd2 f3#.**

(436)
29…c5+ wins the Rook on d5 with discovered check.

(437)
35…Bd1 pins the White Queen to the King.

(438)
12…Qxh2#

(439)
3…g6 protects the pawn, and prevents the checkmate: **4.Bxh5 Rxh5 5.Qxh5 g6 6.Qxg6#.** In the game Black played **3…g5??** and got mated in this manner.

(440)
28…Bd5+ A remove the defender tactic: **29.Kc3 Ne4+ 30.Kd3 Qxb4** winning the White Rook.

(441)
14.Qxd8#

(442)
14…Nxd4 snatches a pawn. If **15.cxd4 Bxd4+ 16.Kh1 Bxa1** Black wins two pawns and a Rook for a Bishop and Knight.

(443)
10.Nb5 threatens **11.Nc7+** and also **11.b4** forking the Black Queen and Bishop. Black cannot meet both threats.

(444)
17…Rxh2+ A nice Rook sacrifice leading to mate: **18.Kxh2 Qh8+ 19.Bh3 Qxh3+ 20.Kg1 Nxe2#,** or **18.Kg1 Nxf3#.**

(445)
10…Bg3# calls in the wolf.

(446)
7.Bf7# The complete game went: 1.e4 e5 2.Nf3 f6 3.d4 d6 4.Bc4 Ne7 5.dxe5 fxe5 6.Nxe5 g6 7.Bf7#.

(447)
8.Bxf7+ Kd8 9.Ne6# A cute checkmate.

(448)
15...Qd7 or *15...Qc8* and Black mates White on the light squares: *16.Nd2 Qh3 17.Nxf3 exf3* and White cannot stop *18...Qg2#.*

(449)
60...Ng2+ forks King and Bishop trading down into an easily won endgame: *61.Kf2 Nxe1 62.Kxe1 d2+* and Black promotes to a Queen on the next move.

(450)
24...Bxh2+ leads to mate: *25.Qxh2 Qxh2+ 26.Kf1 Bd3+ 27.Ke1 Qe2#.*

(451)
18.f4 attacks and wins the Knight, which is pinned to the mate threat on g7. Black cannot move the Knight without allowing *18...Qg7#.*

(452)
10...Bh4+ Discovered attack, winning the White Queen on the next move.

(453)
21.Nc7+ A clearance and deflection tactic:
21...Qxc7 22.Qe6+ forks the Black King and Rook, *22...Qe7 23.Qxg8+ Kd7 24.Qxa8.*

(454)
41...Bd6 pins the White Rook.

(455)
15...Qxf2+ 16.Kh1 Qxe1#.

(456)
16...Nb4 attacks the White Queen on a6, and threatens a fork on the White King and the Rook on c2. White cannot meet both threats.

(457)
36.Re8+ skewers the Black King and Queen.

(458)
32.Rg7+ X-ray attack on the Black Knight on d7.

(459)
35...Bxe4+ Discovered attack on the White Queen from the Black Rook.

(460)
7.Qh5# A variation on 'the Fool's Mate'.

(461)
35.Rxf5 wins a piece, if *35...Qxe5 36.Rxe5 Rxf1 37.Bxf1.* If *35...Rxf5 36.Qxg3.*

(462)
18.Nc7+ invades with a fork of King and Rook.

(463)
29.c7 and the pawn cannot be stopped.

(464)
16.Bg5 traps the Black Queen. Black will be forced to give up some material to save the Queen. For example: *16...Nf3+ 17.Rxf3 Qg4* or *16...Qxg5 17.Qxg5 Nxd3* giving up the Queen for a Bishop and Knight.

(465)
9.Nxe5 wins a piece that is attacked twice, and only defended once.

(466)
37.fxg5+ wins the Black Bishop with discovered check.

(467)
14...Bg4 traps the White Queen.

(468)
49...e3+ Discovered check, winning the White Bishop.

(469)
31...Bxd1 gets the Black Bishop out of danger, and wins a piece. If *32.Rxd1 Ne2+!!* forks the White King and Queen, and threatens a back rank mate with Rxd1.

(470)
37...Qxf1+ wins a Rook that is attacked twice, and only defended once: *38.Qxf1 Rxf1+.*

(471)
9...Bxh6 overloads the White Queen, who can't recapture, and still guard the Knight on d4: *10.Qxh6 Nxd4* wins a piece.

(472)
13.Nxf6# A cute smothered mate.

(473)
53.Rxa2 stops Black from queening his pawn, before making a Queen of his own.

(474)
17...Nc3+ forks the White Queen and King.

(475)
3...Qxe4+ forks the King and Rook on h1.

(476)
45.Be6+ White gets his Bishop out of danger with check, and can take the Black Knight on g3 the next move.

(477)
17...g6 wins the White Queen: **18.Qxh6 Bg7 19.Qh4 Nxh3+** with a discovered attack on the Queen.

(478)
39.Nxh6! wins a pawn. If **39...Kxh6 40.Rh1+** leads to mate: **40...Qh5 41.Qg5+ Kh7 42.Rxh5#.**

(479)
32.Ne7+ leads to mate: **32...Kc5 33.R8d5#** or **32...Kc7 33.Rc8#.**

(480)
34...c3+ forks the White King and Rook.

(481)
25.d4 attacks the pinned Black Bishop, which can't move without losing the Black Rook on c6.

(482)
8.Bd3 traps the Black Queen.

(483)
23.Nxd6 Qxd6 24.Bxc5 forks the Black Queen and Rook. If **23...Nxe3** White will play **24.fxe3** and Black cannot play **24...Qxd6** because of **25.Bh7+** with a discovered attack, winning the Black Queen.

(484)
30...Rxd6 wins the White Bishop, the e-pawn is pinned.

(485)
20.Rxe8 deflects the Black Queen from the defense of the Knight on f6.

(486)
42...Rh8+ 43.Rh6 Rxh6#

(487)
19.Bg4 skewers the Black Queen and Rook.

(488)
32.Rd8#

(489)
24.Nf7+ forks the Black King and Queen.

(490)
24...Qe3# A Dovetail mate.

(491)
7...Be5 wins the Rook on a1, which cannot move or be defended.

(492)
31...Qd5+ and White cannot stop mate: **32.Qe4 Qxe4 33.Rf3 Qxf3 34.Kg1 Nxh3#** (**34...Qg2#**).

(493)
35...Bb3 forces the White Rook off the fourth rank, **36.Rc3** allowing **36...Bd5+** skewering the White King and Knight. Black wins a piece.

(494)
40.Rxd3 takes a piece threatening a back rank mate, and removing the defender of the Black Rook on c1.

(495)
26...axb5+ Discovered attack on the White Queen.

(496)
12...Qb4+ forks the White King and Bishop.

(497)
20...Ne2+ forks the King and Queen.

(498)
18...Ncxe5 winning a pawn with a discovered attack on the Bishop on b5 and a clearance sacrifice threatening **19...c2,** forking the White Queen and Knight.

(499)
12...g5 traps the White Bishop.

(500)
8...Nd3# is a common mating pattern in the Budapest Gambit. On the previous move White played axb4, 'winning' a Bishop, but missing the smothered mate.

(501)
18...Qxc4 Nothing tricky here. The Bishop is attacked twice, and only defended once.

(502)
30...Ng5+ forks the King and Rook.

(503)
15.Bxb4 Nxb4 and either **16.Nc3** or **16.Nbd2** attacks the Black Bishop on e4, and unpins the a-pawn to the White Rook. Black has two pieces under attack, and cannot save both.

(504)
30.Nfg5# An interesting and unusual checkmate in the middle of the board.

(505)
32...Rxg3+ A surprising and alert check, because Black's Queen is hanging and under attack. The f-pawn is pinned, so it cannot capture the Rook.

(506)
32.e6+, which was missed in the game, checks the King and opens a forking-square on e5 for the White Knight. If **32...fxe6, 33.Ne5+** forks the King and Rook. If **32...Ke7, 33.exf7** and the Black King cannot capture this pawn again because of the Knight fork **34.Ne5+**. White ends up with a dangerous passed pawn on the 7th rank or winning the Black Rook.

(507)
47.Bc3 making sure that Black doesn't make a Queen, even though it means giving up the Knight, which is attacked by the f5-pawn.

(508)
22...Nxe5 winning a pawn, and removing a defender of the Knight, which had a nice outpost on d6. The f4-pawn is pinned to the Queen.

(509)
30...Re1+!! deflects the White Rook on d1. If **31.Rxe1** to get out of check, **31...Qxd4** wins the Queen for the Rook. If **31.Kf2**, then **31...Rxd1**

winning the Rook with an X-Ray tactic where the Black Rook is protected through the White Queen.

(510)
23...Qxh3# White is up a piece, but all of his army is on the Queenside doing nothing, while his King is like Macaulay Culkin in *Christmas – Home Alone*.

(511)
30.Re7 attacks the Bishop on e3, and threatens **31.Bh7+ Kf8 32.Ng6#.** Black cannot meet both threats, and will lose the Bishop, or get checkmated.

(512)
White made a mistake by playing **3.fxe5** and is punished with **3...Qh4+** which picks up the e4-pawn on the next move. The complete game went: 1.e4 e5 2.f4 d5 3.fxe5 Qh4+ 4.Ke2 Qxe4+ 5.Kf2 Bc5+ 6.Kg3 Qxe5+ 7.Kf3 Qh5+ 0-1.

(513)
36...Rb2 adds a second attacker against the very weak g2-pawn, threatening mate: **37.Rg1 a1=Q.** Black has several good moves in this position, including f4, which was played in the game.

(514)
16.Qxh6 White has an unusual lineup of pieces and pawns on the d-file. Qxh6 wins a loose pawn and threatens mate on h7.

(515)
22.Rxe4 wins a piece – the d5-pawn is pinned.

(516)
25...Re2+ 26.Kg1 (or **26.Kf3**) **26...Qxg2#**

(517)
25.Qf8+ forks the Black King and Rook.

(518)
17...Qxb2 gets the Queen out of the attack from the White Knight on g4 and wins a pawn.

(519)
6...Nc2+ Family Fork.

(520)
30.Qc3 pinning the Black Rook to the Black Queen, which is getting overloaded trying to protect h7 and the Rook on f6.

(521)
24...Ba6 skewers the Rook and Bishop.

(522)
28...hxg3 opens up the h-file where Black has a deadly battery lined up. Amazingly White somehow survived this attack, and won the game in a near 600 point upset.

(523)
13.Nd6+ Kd8 14.Nf7+ forks the King and Rook.

(524)
32...Rh1+ Not Rxf2 which was played in the game. It is better to play *32...Rh1+* followed by *33.Kg2 R8h2+ 34.Kg3 Bh4+ 35.Kf4 Rxf2+ 36.Ke5 Rxa1* when Black has won everything, not just the Queen for a Rook.

(525)
15.Be3 and Black cannot stop the mate: *16.Bxa7+ Kxa7 17.Qa6+ Kb8 18.Qa8#.*

(526)
37.gxf4, deflecting the Queen from her protection of the Black Bishop on g7.

(527)
7...Qh4+ forks the White King and Knight.

(528)
38.Rh5+ followed by mate after Kg7 Rh7#.

(529)
12.hxg5, opening up the h-file. See follow up in the next problem.

(530)
13.Qh5 creates a battery on the h-file. These types of attacks against a castled King can be very hard to defend against. In this case there is no way to stop the mate:
13...f5 14.g6 Qh4 15.Rxh4 Nxd2 16.Qh7#
13...f6 14.g6 Nxd2 15.Qh7#
13...Nxd2 14.Qh7#

(531)
22.Rd4 forks the Queen and Knight. The Black Knight is covering e5, and the mate threat of Qe5+. After *22...f4 23.Rxf4 Qd8 24.Rxc4* Black cannot take as there is a threat *25.Qe5+*, Black has to play *24...Rg6 25.Qe5+ Kg8 26.Rg4!* and White is a piece up.

(532)
36.Nc6+ and Black has to give up the Rook, or gets hook mated with *36...Kb6* or *36...Kb7 37.Rb8#.*

(533)
52...f2 and the White Rook cannot stop a pawn from queening.

(534)
9...Bxf3 removes the defender of the g5-square: *10.gxf3 Bg5* pinning the White Queen to the King. This is a common tactic when one side has castled Queenside.

(535)
47.Rg7+!! Discovered attack on the Black Queen on f5.

(536)
24.Bxd4 and if *24...Qxd4 25.Bb5+* with a discovered attack.

(537)
47.Qc4+ forks the Black King and Rook.

(538)
16...Nc3+ forks the White King and Rook.

(539)
12.Bxd5 exd5 13.Bxe7 Rxe7 14.Nxd5 forks the Black Queen and Rook (the c-pawn is pinned).

(540)
50.c7 The only winning move, *50...Rc6 51.Rd7* and Black can't stop *Rd8+* and *c8=Q.*

(541)
12...Nf4 forks the White Queen and Bishop. The Queen cannot move, and still protect the Bishop.

(542)
13...Qg3+ A forced mate on the weak dark squares: *14.Kf1 Be3 15.Nh3 Bxh3 16.Rxh3 Qf2#.*

(543)
33.Re6+!! On the previous move Black played 32...Rh7?? hoping for 33.Rxh7 Kxf6 with an even trade, but missed this move. If *33...fxe6 34.Rxh7+* skewering the Black King and the Black Knight on b7, winning a piece. If the Black King moves to get out of check, then simply *34.Rxh7* and the g7-pawn is pinned to the Knight.

(544)
22...Rxf4 wins a piece with a discovered attack on the White Queen.

(545)
34...bxc4 gets the King out of check, and captures a Bishop that is just hanging there. Problems like this are kind of 'stupid' but good at training you to really look at what is going on in the position, and not miss the 'obvious'. They often have surprisingly low success rates on tactics trainers' sites where you can see how well people did in solving a problem.

(546)
67...Nd8 The only move for Black here. This stops the f6-pawn from advancing to make a Queen, and makes it awkward for the White Bishop to get back in the game without sacrificing his best pawn. Black went on to win this game in 85 moves.

(547)
24.Qxc3 picks up the hanging piece. The overly complicated **24.Bxh6??**, hoping for **25.Qxg7#**, loses to **24...Ne2+** forking the White King and Queen.

(548)
39...Qd4+ forks the White Rook and King. **40.Rc3 b4** attacking the pinned piece.

(549)
19...Bh4 pins the White Queen to the King.

(550)
28.Qxe8+ The crowning sacrifice: **28...Kxe8 29.h8=Q+**.

(551)
44...b5 traps and discovers an attack on the White Bishop.

(552)
9.e6 attacks the pinned Black Bishop on d7 and discovers an attack on the g7-pawn from the White Bishop on c3. Black cannot defend both threats.

(553)
43.Kd3 prevents **43...Be4** stopping the runaway h-pawn, and gives White an easy win.

(554)
24.Nxe5 The best move here is to ignore the threat to your Queen, and create a threat of your own with this capture. **24...Rxd3 25.Nxc6** and White is up a piece.

(555)
31.Rxe7+ and it is 'Good Night to you' **31...Nxe7 32.Qxe7+** forks the King and Rook.

(556)
17...Be4 skewers the Queen and Rook.

(557)
16.Rfc1 kicks the Queen, so White can safely play **17.Qxd5** on the next move, winning a piece.

(558)
19.Be5 Fritz notated this move with 'and White can celebrate victory'. This adds a second attacker to the Black Knight on g3. If **19...Nf5 20.g4** forks the two Knights.

(559)
22.Bc2 traps the Queen forcing Black to give up material.

(560)
22...Rg6 traps the White Bishop.

(561)
31.Qd8+ Houston, we have a problem: **31...Rxd8 32.Rxd8#**.

(562)
22.Qxd4+ grabs a piece, and skewers the Black King and Rook.

(563)
7.Ne5 Black's Kingside has more holes than a block of Swiss cheese. White threatens **Bf7#** and **Qh5+** leading to mate. Black will have to give up material with moves such as **7...Ng6** to avoid a forced mate.

(564)
32...Rc1#

(565)
28...Nc4 The only safe square for the Knight on e5, which is under attack.

(566)
13.Bc5 attacks the Black Rook on f8 defending the f7-pawn, which has no good squares to move to.

(567)
31...Qe3+ forks the White King and Rook.

(568)
38...Rf3#

(569)
14.Nb6!! A clearance sacrifice, threatening the Black Rook on a8, and threatening mate with Qf7#.

(570)
34.Qa2+ gets the White Queen to a safe square with check. After Black gets out of check, for example 34...Kh7, White plays 35.hxg3, and is up a piece. With this check, White buys time to save his Queen, and capture the Rook on g3.

(571)
41...Rd1+ nails it down. *42.Re1* (only way to get out of check) *42...Rxe1 43.Kxe1 fxg2* and White cannot stop Black from queening. Playing *42... fxg2+* overloading the White King also wins.

(572)
8.a5 overloads the Black Queen. If *8...Nxa5 9.Bxb2 Qxb2 10.Rxa5* and White wins a Knight for 2 pawns. If *8...Qb4 9.c3* and Black has no safe squares where he can still guard the Bishop on b2.

(573)
10.d5 is a common pawn fork.

(574)
20.Qc8+ and a back rank mate after *20...Qd8 21.Qxd8+ Ne8 22.Rxe8#* (or *22.Qxe8#*).

(575)
21.Qxc8! leading to a Knight fork: *21...Qxc8 22.Ne7+* winning a Rook.

(576)
42...Nh4+ forks the King and Queen (the g3-pawn is pinned, so cannot capture the Knight).
A good example of ignoring threats to your own pieces (the hanging Queen on g4) and finding threats of your own to make.

(577)
14. ...Nc2 forks the White Rooks.

(578)
14...Rh1+!! and mate after *15.Kxh1 Qh4 16.Kg1 Qh2#:* This is a very good mating pattern to know.

(579)
15.Qd7+ delivers Black pain. The Knight cannot capture the White Queen because of the pin from the Bishop on g5. *15...Kf8 16.Qxf7#.*

(580)
20...Nf3+ is a common mating pattern with 'Fishing Pole' style formation attacks. After *21.gxf3 exf3* Black has a discovered attack from the Bishop on g6 to the Queen on c2, and a mating net with Qh3 and Qg2#. White cannot stop both threats.

(581)
8.e5 attacks the Knight on d6 and clears the way for the mating attack with Bishop and Queen on h7. Black cannot meet both threats at the same time, and will either lose a piece, or be mated. Attacks like these are common in scholastic tournaments.

(582)
22...Qxf2# On the previous move White played 22.Rh1?? trying to harass the Queen, but should have defended the f2-pawn instead with 22.Rf1.

(583)
22...Qxd2# A nice checkmate. Black lost a piece early in the game, but survived an attack, fought back, and punished White for leaving his King in the middle of the board.

(584)
White has two pieces hanging (the Knight on h8 and the Bishop on c5), but *18.Ng6* leads to an amazing mate in 2: *18...Ke8 19.Nd6#.*

(585)
11...Nc2+ is a common forking-square for the Knight.

(586)
20.f5 leaves Black with no good defenses. His Queen is under attack, and is needed for the defense of the Knight on f6, which is attacked

twice by White. There are no squares where the Black Queen can move, and still defend the Black Knight.

(587)
13...Nd4 attacks the Knight on f3, which is preventing the mate Qxh2#, and also threatens Ne2+. If **14.cxd4 Bxd4+** leads to mate.

(588)
20...Nd3 forks the White Queen and Rook. The White Bishop on e2 cannot capture the Knight, because it is threat pinned to the Rook on e1, due to the battery of Black Rooks on the e-file.

(589)
22.Nxd6 forks the Black Queen and Rook.

(590)
24...exf4 attacking the Black Bishop, if **25.Bxf4 Bxf4 26.Nxf4 Nf2** forking the White Rooks. Same idea with **25.Nxf4 Bxf4 26.Bxf4 Nf2**: if the Bishop moves, **25...f3** discovered check attacking the White Knight on e2.

(591)
29...Rh1# A typical mate with two Rooks.

(592)
19...Rd8 pinning and adding a second attacker to the White Bishop on the Queen. **19...Rd7** is not as good because of **20.Qa4.**

(593)
20.Bxf4 takes a piece that is just sitting there.

(594)
13...Qa5+ forks the White King and the Knight on f5, winning a piece. **14.Kf1 Qxf5.**

(595)
22.Rxb6 Qxb6 23.d5 discovers an attack on the Queen, winning the Bishop on the next move. White wins two Bishops for a Rook.

(596)
6.Bb5 pins the Black Queen to the King.

(597)
21...Rd8 adds a second attacker to the White Knight and pins it to the Queen. **22. Nce2 e5** wins the pinned Knight.

(598)
22...Bg5 A discovered attack on the Queen, and an X-Ray attack on the White Bishop on e3. After the Queen moves, Black will win the Bishop. For example **23.Qxb4 Rxe3.**

(599)
19...Ng3#.

(600)
15...Bc3+ 16.Qc2 The only way to get out of check. **16...Bxd2** wins the Queen for a Bishop.

(601)
21...Nxe4+ forks the White King and pinned Knight.

(602)
14.Bg7 forks the Black Rook and Knight, which is now attacked twice.

(603)
9...e5 forks the White Queen and Bishop.

604)
27.Ng5+ Discovered check leading to mate: **27...e6 28.Qxe6+ Kg7 29.Qf7+ Kh6 30.Qxh7+ Kxg5 31.Qh4#. Or 27...Kf8 28.Qf7#.**

(605)
90...Qb1+ forks the White King and Queen, forcing a trade of Queens. After **91.Qe4 Qxe4 92.Kxe4 a2** Black will win the race to Queen his pawn.

(606)
12...Bb7 traps the White Queen.

(607)
9.Qxc5 wins the Bishop, the Black Knight is pinned to the King.

(608)
31...Rxc1#

(609)
9.Bxf7+ Kxf7 10.Nxe5+ Kg8 11.Qxg4 wins two pawns for White.

(610)
34.Nc6+ forks the Black King and the Bishop on e5. The Bishop on d7 is pinned.

(611)
7...Qxe4+ and mate the next move: *8.Qe2 Qxe2.*

(612)
61...Rxf5+ The knockout blow. *62.Kxf5 Kxe7* and Black trades into an easily won endgame.

(613)
13.Nxe7+ Qxe7 14.Bxd6 wins a pawn, and skewers the Black Queen and Rook.

(614)
32.Qf7+ Kh8 33.Qxg7#

(615)
29...Bf5 pins the White Knight to the King. If *30.Rb4* to guard the Knight, *30...Re8* attacks the Bishop, and X-ray attacks the Knight. White cannot meet both threats, and will lose a piece.

(616)
11.Qxd8 gets the White Queen out of danger, and buys time to play *12.exf6* winning the Black Knight.

(617)
25.Be4+ leads to mate: *25...f5 26.Bxf5 g6 27.Rh8#.* A good mate pattern to know with Bishop and Rook.

(618)
27.Nc4+!! A brilliant mate in 2 forking the Black King and Queen, and deflecting the Black Knight: *27...Nxc4 28.Rd7#.*

(619)
8.Qa4+ Double attack, picking up the bishop on g4, which is looser than a thrift store turtleneck.

(620)
30...Rh3 and White cannot stop *...Rxh2#* or *...Qxh2#.*

(621)
48.Qxc7+ Rxc7 49.Rb7 and White transitions into an easily won endgame. He will either win the a-pawn on the next move, or if 49...Rxb7 50.axb7 he will get a Queen on the next move.

(622)
6.Bxf7+ wins a pawn with a common opening trick, *6...Kxf7 7. Ne5+ Ke8 8.Qxg4.*

(623)
31...Qe2 and White cannot protect the Rook, and prevent Qxd3# or Qc1#: *32.Rd2 Qxd2 33.Qc3 Qd1+ 34.Qc1 Qxc1#.*

(624)
24...Nxa2# Smothered mate with White surrounded by useless pieces.

(625)
54.e7 and Black cannot stop a White pawn from queening. The game continued *54...Nxe7 55.Nxe7 h2 56.c8=Q h1=Q 57.Qg8+* resigns. White will trade Queens, then make another Queen.

(626)
26...Rxg4 wins a Rook – the h-pawn is pinned.

(627)
18.Qxc6 wins a piece; if *18...Qxc6 19.Ne7+* forking the Black King and Queen.

(628)
20.Qf6+!! got a double exclam from Deep Rybka. The e-pawn is pinned: *20...exf6 Rxe8#* (or *20...Kg8 Qg7#*).

(629)
21...Qxh3+ The g-pawn is pinned. *22.Kg1 Qxg2#.*

(630)
31...Bd4+ forks the King and Rook.

(631)
20.Nf6+ Double discovered check – after *20...Kh8* White follows up with *21.Bxh6* and mate soon after. For example *21...Nxf6 22. exf6 Bxf6 23.Bf4+ Kg8 24.Qh7#.*

(632)
14.Bxf7+ nails it down: *14...Kxf7 15.Qc4+ Kf8 16.Bc7* traps the Black Queen.

(633)
42.b7 and the White pawn cannot be stopped from becoming a Queen.

(634)
27.Bxc4 wins a piece that is attacked three times, but only defended once. Nothing tricky here.

(635)
26.Nxe5+ grabs a pawn, and wins the Black Queen with a discovered check.

(636)
19.Qg6+ leads to mate with the idea **19...Kh8 20.Qxh6+ Kg8 21.Kh2** and the White Rook checkmates on the open g-file.

(637)
30...Kg7 with the threat Rh8 leads to mate: **31.Bg8 Rxg8 32.Kh3 Rh8+ 33.Nh6 Rxh6+ 34.Qh5 Rxh5#.**

(638)
34...Nf3+ and White has to give up the Queen to get out of check: **35.Qxf3 Qxf3.**

(639)
25...Bxg3 threatens mate and attacks the Rook on e1. White is busted. Some sample lines:
26.Rc2 (to stop Qxh2+ and Qf2#) **Bxe1 27.Qxe1 Qxf3** and Black is up a Bishop and two pawns.
26.Qe2 Rxe3 27.Qg2 Rxe1+ 28.Rxe1 Bxe1, White is down two Bishops.
26.Re2 Bxf3 pinning the Rook to the Queen, and grabbing another pawn.

(640)
22...Bxe4 23.Qxe4 Nxg3 forks the Queen and Rook. The f-pawn cannot capture because of the pin from the Black Queen. Black comes out ahead a pawn, and the exchange.

(641)
34.Qxb8+!! got a double exclam from Deep Rybka. This move wins a piece, and forks the King and Queen. After **34...Qxb8 35.Ra8** pins the Queen to the King. If **35...Qxa8 36.bxa8=Q+** forks the King and Rook.

(642)
33.Rh8+! Kxh8 34.Qf8+ Kh7 35.Rh1+ Nh6 36.Ng5#

(643)
42.Rxd4 overloads the Black Bishop, which can't protect both the Rook and pawn on f4.

(644)
54.e6 –saving the pawn is more important than saving the Bishop. Black cannot stop White from making a Queen.

(645)
6.Qh5+ g6 7.Qxg6+!! hxg6 8.Bxg6# (or the less dramatic **7.Bxg6 hxg6 8.Qxg6#**).

(646)
20.Bxh7+ is an alert in between move. Both the White Queen and Black Queen are under attack. If **20...Kxh7 21.Qh3+** and White moves his Queen out of danger with check, and Black will lose his Queen on the next move.

(647)
9...Nxd4 wins a piece.

(648)
42.Qe7 threatens the Rook on e8, threatens mate on g7, and protects the passed pawn on a7. If **42...Rxe7 43.a8=R+** leads to mate. If **42...Rg8** to guard the mate threat, White still Queens, with **43.a8=R** (or **43.a8=Q**), and Black cannot stop mate.

(649)
18.Bg6+ and mate after **18...Nh6 19.Bxh6 Rf7 20.Bxg7+ Kxg7 21.Qh7+ Kf8 22.Qxf7#.**

(650)
32.Bxc4 takes advantage of the pinned b-pawn. If **32...dxc4 33.d5!** Discovered attack on the Black Rook and Queen. If **32...Rxc4 33.Rxc4 dxc4 34.d5** kicks the Black Queen off the weak dark squares and **35.Qc3** will lead to mate.

(651)
16...Be6 overloads the Rook and skewers the Rook and Bishop. If **17.Rc5 Bxe5 18.Bxe6 Bf4+ 19.Kd1 fxe6** and Black is up a piece.

(652)
33...Qe2#

(653)
15...Nxc4 takes the White Bishop with a discovered attack from the Black Bishop on g7 to the White Knight on c3. White cannot recapture, and protect the Knight, and will lose a piece. For example **16.Bxc4 Bxc3.** These types of discovered attacks are very common and this is a good pattern to know.

(654)
16.Nxc6+ discovers an attack on the Black Queen with check. After **16...Qxc6 17.Qxa7+ Kc7** (or **17...Kc8**) **18.Rc3** pins the Black Queen to the King.

(655)

16...Bxc1 wins a piece. If *17.Rxc1* then *17...Qg5* forks the King and Rook.

(656)

15...Qxb2!! wins a pawn that appears to be protected and attacks the Rook on a1, which cannot be defended. The Black Queen cannot be taken because of the back rank mate threat *16...Rd1#.* Very alert play by Black.

(657)

31.Rxe6+ leads to a long, forced mate: *31...Kxe6 32.Re1+ Kd6* (32...Kf6 33.Qe7+ Kg6 34.Re6#) *33.Qe7+ Kc6 34.Qc5+ Kd7 35.Re7+ Kd8 36.Qd6+ Qd7 37.Qxd7#.*

(658)

38...Rc1+ 39. Ka2 Qxa4+ 40.Ra3 Qc4+ forks the King and Rook.

(659)

13.Bxc6 removes the defender of the Black Queen on a5. After *13...Qxd2 14.Bxd7+* (in between move) *14...Kxd7 15.Bxd2* White is up a piece. The key is to play the checking move before recapturing the piece. The White Bishop has already captured one piece. Then Black takes the White Queen, then White takes a second piece with the Bishop that is a check – THEN he recaptures the Queen. Combinations like this in blitz can happen so fast that sometimes you don't even realize that you lost a piece. The move order is important.

(660)

12...Bg4+ skewering the White King and Queen, and removing the King from the defense of the White Bishop on d3.

(661)

31.Rh3 threatening *32.Ng6+ fxg6 33.Qxh7#* which Black has no good way to stop.

(662)

38.Nxf7# Black has a Knight, Rook and Queen all guarding the King, but they are no match for the White Knight and the deathly pawn duo.

(663)

23...f6 doubly attacking both the White Bishop on g5 with the f6-pawn and the White Queen on

h5 from the Black Bishop on e8. White can't save both, and Black wins a piece.

(664)

26...Qh1 and there are no safe squares for the White Rook to go to.

(665)

8.Bg6+! hxg6 9.Qxg6#, or
8.Qg6+! hxg6 9.Bxg6#

(666)

50.h7 and White will win the pawn race.

(667)

30.f4 gets White out of check, and attacks the Black Queen who is starting to get overloaded. White wants to play Rxf7# and Black will have a hard time stopping down all of the threats from White. For example if *30...Qf6 31.Qxd6+* and the Black Queen cannot capture White's Queen and continue to guard f7 at the same time.

(668)

18...Bxh2+ Discovered attack on the Queen on e3.

(669)

20...Qd5 forks the two Rooks.

(670)

29.Qh8+!! is the type of move you see in a typical tactics book. White gives up his Queen to deflect the Black King, and mate on the next move if Black captures with a promotion to another Queen, *29...Kxh8 30.exf8Q#*. If the King docsn't take, White gets two Queens, and mates a few moves later.

(671)

54.Re5+ Forks the King and Knight. Black had to sacrifice his Knight on the previous move, to grab a runaway pawn on h5.

(672)

4.Qxf7#. The classic '4 move checkmate'.

(673)

20.Rab1 kicks the Queen off of the b-file. After the Queen moves, *21.Rb8+* skewers the King and the Black Rook on h8, *21...Ke7 22.Rxh8.*

(674)
21.b5 traps the Bishop on a6.

(675)
46...Kg5 traps the White Rook. The King makes a good offensive weapon in the endgame. Players often turn their 'tactics radar' off in the endgame, but this is a mistake.

(676)
10.Nf5 discovers an attack on the Black Queen on b6 and the Black Bishop on g7 at the same time.

(677)
29...Qb2+ The dark squares are weaker than Popeye without spinach for White. Black mates with *29...Qb2+ 30.Kd1 Rd8+ 31.Qd4 cxd4 32.e4 Rc8 33.Ke1 Rc1#.*

(678)
26...Bxh3 White just sacrificed the Knight on g7, planning to undermine the defense of the Knight on f6. The problem is this leaves his Bishop on h3 under-defended. This move also attacks the Rook on f1. If *27.Qxf6 Rc6* and the White Queen cannot protect the White Knight on g7. Black is now attacking the White Knight on g7 and the White Rook on f1, and cannot save all at the same time. Black wins material.

(679)
28.N7f5 clears the way for *29.Qg7#* and also threatens *29.Nh6#.* Black cannot meet all of these threats.

(680)
35.Qd6+ White sacrificed material to build this mating net, and finishes it off with *35.Qd6+ Kc8* (only move) *36.Bxe6#* ruining Black's 'summer vacation'.

(681)
19...Rae8 adds a second attacker to the Bishop on e4. This Bishop is 'threat pinned', which is a term coined by Life Master Joel Johnson. The Bishop can't move because of …Rxe1+ forking the King and Queen. Black can play f5 on the next move to take advantage of this pin.

(682)
35...Rh5# and White is mated, with a sideways back rank mate.

(683)
64...Qe4+ and mate to follow:
65.Qf3 Qxf3+ 66.Kg1 Qg2#
65.Kg1 Qg2#

(684)
35...Nf2+ leads to an attractive mate: *36.Rxf2 Qa1+ 37.Bd1 Rxd1 38.Qxd1 Qxd1 39.Rf1 Qxf1#* or the 'Philidor's Legacy' with *36.Kg1 Nh3+ 37.Kh1 Qg1+ 38.Rxg1 Nf2#* smothered mate.

(685)
30...Bxg3 if *31.fxg3 f2+* forks the King and Rook. Pawn forks like this can be hard to spot.

(686)
22.Qxe7 wins a piece – if *22...Qxe7 23.Ng6+* forks the King and Queen.

(687)
20.Bb5+ This nice move accomplishes several things – it deflects and attacks the Black Bishop that is on a4 attacking the Queen on b3 (with check), and clears the e-file, preparing the move Rfe1 pinning the Queen to the King. Black cannot deal with all these threats at the same time, and will lose material.

(688)
White ignores the threat to his own Bishop, which is under attack, and goes on the offense with *23.Qd7+* which forks the Black King and Bishop. The Bishop cannot block the check because the e7-square is also attacked by the Rook on e1. Fritz 13 points out several forced mates:
1. +- (#5): 23...Kg8 24.Bh6 Qc7 25.Re8+ Bf8 26.Qxd5+ Qf7 27.Rxa8 Qxd5 28.Rxf8#
2. +- (#3): 23...Be7 24.Rxe7+ Kg8 25.Qxd5+ Kf8 26.Qf7#
3. +- (#2): 23...Kf8 24.Bh6+ Kg8 25.Qe6#
4. +- (#1): 23...Kf6 24.Re6#

(689)
10.Bxd7 White wants to play b4 to trap the Knight, but needs to liquidate the Bishop first. After *10.Bxd7 Qxd7 11.b4* traps the Knight. Knights on the rim are vulnerable to being trapped, because they have so few escape-squares.

(690)
33.Rg8 cuts off the Black King, brings another attacker in, and threatens mate with Qh4. Fritz 13 points out a forced mate after *33.Rg8 Kh5 34.g4+ Bxg4 35.hxg4+ Kh4 36.Qf4 Qg6 37.g5+ Kh5 38.Be2#* (although I didn't expect you to see this).

(691)
19.b4 traps the Queen like R. Kelly in the closet. Black played *18...Nb6??* on the previous move helpmating his own Queen. Even 2000+ rated players make these types of mistakes.

(692)
30.Bxd1 The obvious way to get out of check, and White will mate soon after *30.Bxd1 fxg6 31.Bb3+ Bd5 32.Bxd5+ Rf7 33.Bxf7+ Kf8 34.Bd6#*.

(693)
23.e6 is a discovered attack. If *23...Bxe6 24.Bxg7 Kxg7 25.Qxa4*.

(694)
36.Bxb6 wins a pawn that appears to be defended. The a-pawn is pinned to the Rook on a8, and the Queen cannot capture because of Rxb6.

(695)
On the previous move Black played *18...g6* hoping to kick the Queen, but *19.exf7+* ignores this threat, and causes problems for the Black King. The f7-square is attacked 3 times and only defended twice. Always be on the lookout for ways that you can attack instead of doing an automatic retreat.

(696)
24.Qg5#

(697)
24.b7#

(698)
22.Qxf8# Black wasted a lot of time in this game making pawn moves, and losing tempi with his Queen, instead of developing and getting his King to safety.

(699)
25...f5 deflects the White Knight from the defense of the White Bishop on g3.

(700)
22...Bxd4+ forks the White King and Knight.

(701)
28.Bc5+ skewers the Black King and Rook.

(702)
8.Bxc4 Black took a pawn on c4 on the previous move, leaving his Queen to be taken, which it was.

(703)
24...Qe6 and White cannot stop mate. For example *25...Qh3+ 26.Kg1 Qg2#*.

(704)
17...Ne3+ forks the White King and Queen.

(705)
36.Rf8+!! If *36...Kxf8 37.Qd8#*, if *36...Kh7 37.Qg4* leads to mate, with the immediate threat *38.Qg6#*.

(706)
23.Rxf6+ deflects the Black King from the defense of the Rook on f8.

(707)
25.Rh6 and Black cannot stop the mate threat Rh8#.

(708)
30.Rd8#

(709)
24.Ra8+ Qxa8 25.Qxa8#

(710)
24.Ra7 wins the Black Queen, who can't move without giving up checkmate, or giving more material. If *24...Qc6 25.Ne5*.

(711)
19...Nd3 forks the White Queen, Rook and Bishop.

(712)
9...Ng4 attacks the e3-pawn, which cannot be defended. It also threatens the Knight Fork of Queen and Rook. This is a common weak point in openings like the Bird, and the Stonewall.

(713)
30...Qxc1 takes the unprotected White Rook.

(714)
26...Rb8 Pin it, and win it. The White Knight is attacked for a second time, and pinned to the White Queen, and cannot be defended a second time.

(715)
34...Nxd2+ takes the Rook, and forks the White King and Rook.

(716)
42.Qg8+ Kh6 43.Qg6# White is down a piece, but makes a nice comeback win.

(717)
21...Qxe5 picks up a hanging piece.

(718)
29...Bh6 skewers the Black Queen and Rook.

(719)
28...Ne3 forking the two White Rooks.

(720)
17.Nxb6+ Discovered attack, which wins the Queen on e6: **17...axb6 18.Qxe6+.**

(721)
15...cxd5 attacks the White Bishop, which can't move without exposing the undefended Knight on c3: **16.Be2 Qxc3.**

(722)
15.e5 with a double discovered attack on the Knight and Queen.

(723)
12...Nd4 attacks the White Queen, chasing it to a bad square. Sample lines:
13.Qd1 Nxd3+ 14.Kf1 Nxc1
13.Qe4 (or **13.Qf1**) **Nxc2+**
13.Qf2 Nxd3+ forking the King and Queen with double discovered check.

(724)
30.Bh7+ leads to a forced mate: **30.Bh7+ Kh8 31.Bg6+ Kg8 32.Qh7+ Kf8 33.Qh8+ Ke7 34.Qxd8#**
The Bishop gives a check first, forcing the King to the corner, then moves to g6 with a discovered check blocking out the Rook on g3 from its defensive duties. This type of maneuver is often used to mate the King with Qf7+, but that isn't possible here because of the Black Bishop on e6, but is a really good mating pattern to know. Note that the Rook on d4 is pinned by the Black Queen, but still helps out in the end.

(725)
49.d7 overloads the Black Knight who cannot stop both runaway passed pawns: **49...Nxd7 50.a8=Q.**

(726)
11.Bxa6 White has the textbook perfect development, and simply takes a piece that is attacked twice and defended once.

(727)
17...Qxd4 and Black wins a piece. If **18.Qxd4 Nxe2+.**

(728)
14.Bd4 attacks the trapped Rook on h8, which has no safe squares.

(729)
19.Bf7# Always check, it might be mate!

(730)
21.Bg8 clears the way for the White Queen to mate: **21...Kxg8 22.Qh7+ Kf8 23.Qh8#**
21...Rxg8 (or any other move) **22.Qh7#**

(731)
18...Bxf2+ wins a valuable pawn helping to protect the White King. If **19.Kxf2 Qxe4** because the White Bishop on f3 is now pinned.

(732)
17.Rxe5 is a kill shot that trades a Rook for two Knights, and puts the Queen on a dangerous square. **17...Nxe5 18.Qxe5** and Black cannot stop the mate threats and defend threats such as **19.Bg5** forking the Black Queen and Black Rook.

(733)
19.Qxc7# The ending from the previous position.

(734)
20.f6+ forks the Black King and Bishop.

(735)
38...Rf2# with an interesting double Knight Mate.

(736)
17.Qh7# A common mating pattern with the battery of Queen and Bishop.

(737)
24...Nf3 threatens **25...Qg1#.**
If **25.Bd3 Rxd3**, and White cannot recapture because of **26...Qg1#.** If **25.gxf3 Qxf3** forks the King and Rook.

(738)
16.Bxf6 removes the defender of the h7-square. If **16...Bxf6 17.Qh7#**, which is what happened in the game.

(739)
39...Bxc5+ grabs a piece, and forks the White King and Rook.

(740)
9...Qxh4 grabs the misplaced White Knight.

(741)
26.g5 attacks the Black Bishop: **26...hxg5 27.fxg5,** if **27...Bxg5 28.Qxg7+** forks the Black King and Bishop.

(742)
22.Qxg7#

(743)
13...h6 14.Bf4 g5 forks the White Bishop and Knight.

(744)
17...Rfg8 traps the White Queen.

(745)
19...Qd4 forks the White Rook and Bishop on f4.

(746)
19...Qd4+ forks the White King and Rook.

(747)
31...Qxe4+ wins a Rook: **32.dxe4 Rxd8.**

(748)
31...Ne2+ forks the White King and Rook.

(749)
35...Qxb2+ 36.Qxb2 Bxb2 37.Kb1 Rxd2 wins a Rook.

(750)
26...Bd3 pins the White Rook to the King.

(751)
27.Rxh6+ leads to mate: **27...Kxh6** (only move) **28.Rh3#.**

(752)
8...Rb8 punishes Black for grabbing a poisoned pawn. **9.Qa6** (only safe square) **9...Nb4** attacking the Queen and the weak c2-square. **10.Qxa7 Nxc2+** forking the White King and Rook.

(753)
13.Nxe7+ Rxe7 14.Bxe5 dxe5 15.Nxe5 wins a pawn.

(754)
39.Qf6+ forks the Black King and Queen: **39...Qxf6 40.exf6+** forking the Black King and Rook.

(755)
28.Rxg6 removes the defender of the e7-square. **28...fxg6 29.Ne7+** forking the Black King and Queen.

(756)
29...Rxf3 30.gxf3 Qxe3 and Black wins two Knights for the Rook, and weakens the White Kingside.

(757)
30.Bxd5+ forks the Queen and King while grabbing a pawn.

(758)
34...Rxd5 White thought he could leave the Bishop hanging because of the back rank mate threat but it doesn't work: **35.Rc8+ Rd8.**

(759)
33.Bf8# Discovered check and mate.

(760)
10.Kxh4 takes the Queen after the really horrible blunder **9...Qh4+??** on the previous move, which just hangs the Queen. Stuff like this actually happens in rated long time control games with good players. Never trust that your opponent's last move wasn't a terrible blunder!

(761)
12.Nb5 threatening both **13.Nc6+** forking the King and Rook and **13.Rab1** trapping the Black Queen. Black cannot deal with both threats.

(762)
38.Qh8#

(763)
18.Bxg7 wins a pawn. Black can't capture the Bishop because of **18...Kxg7 19.Ne6+** which would fork the Black King and Queen. This move also clears a square for the White Queen to enter the attack. **18.Ne6** forking the Queen and Rook is also a good move, and was played in the game.

(764)
19.Bxe6+ wins a pawn with check, forking the Black King and Rook.

(765)
32.Rxd4 wins a piece. If **32...Rxd4 33.Nxb5+** forking the Black King and Rook.

(766)
22...Ng3 forks the White Queen and Rook, taking advantage of the pinned f-pawn. Black wins the exchange.

(767)
21.Nxf6+ takes advantage of the overloaded Black Queen who is trying to guard both the Knight on f6 and the Bishop on c7, and can't do both.

(768)
39.Nf5 takes advantage of the limited mobility of the Black Rook on e7. If **39...Re6 40.Ng7** forks the two Rooks. White wins the exchange.

(769)
54.Be4+ forks the Black King and Rook.

(770)
15...Qxf3 Black's Queen was attacked by the White Knight. After **16.gxf3 Nxc5** and Black is up a piece.

(771)
30.Qxf8+!! got a well-deserved double exclam from Deep Rybka 4.1. **30...Kxf8 31.Re8#** is a good mating pattern to know.

(772)
17...Qg4#

(773)
22.Bg4 pins the Black Queen to the King.

(774)
15...Qxa5 grabs a piece that is attacked twice, and defended once.

(775)
16.b3 traps the Black Bishop who grabbed a poisoned pawn.

(776)
42...Qxh3#

(777)
41...Na3 forks the Queen and Rook.

(778)
17...Rh8 skewers the Queen and Knight: **18.Qg7 Rxh5.**

(779)
16...Nxd5 White thought he had a discovered attack, winning a pawn with 16.Nxd5?? but **16...Nxd5** captures the Knight, protecting the Black Bishop on b4.

(780)
28.Qd4+ and Black will have to give up the Knight to get out of check, **28...Nf6 29.Qxf6.**

(781)
28...Rxd1 29.Rxd1 Bxf3+ forks the King and Rook. Starting off with **28...Bxf3+** works also.

(782)
8.Qxg7 taking a pawn, threatening the Black Rook on h8, and check on f7. Black has no good way to deal with all these problems.

(783)
28.Rxe7 takes the Bishop, and deflects the Black Queen from the defense of the Rook on g4, **28...Qxe7 29.Qxg4.**

(784)
18.Bxf8. White has several reasonable moves to consider, but taking the Rook is best, because it also attacks the Queen. **18...Kxf8 19.Qxd3**, and White is up a Rook.

(785)
16...Bf5 A surprising move that punishes the early development of the White Queen. There are no good squares for the Queen. Black is threatening **17...g6** trapping the Queen. If **17.Qf3 Be4** skewers the Queen and Rook.

(786)
10...Qxe5 Black played a useful forking check on the previous move, and collects his winnings here. This is a good pattern to know.

(787)
22...Rg2+ 23.Kh1 Qxh3 is a nice mate in two.

(788)
5.Nxf7 A common tactic in the Fried Liver Attack, winning a pawn, and forking the Black Queen and Rook.

(789)
14...Bb4+ leads to a surprising opening checkmate: **15.Nc3 Bxc3+ 16.Bd2 Qxd2+ 17.Kf1 Bh3+ 18.Kg1 Qg5#**, or **15.Kf1 Bh3+ 16.Kg1 Qd1#**.

(790)
34.Rd7#

(791)
7.Bg5 traps the Black Queen.

(792)
15.Ng4+ wins the Queen with a discovered check.

(793)
7...Bxa3 8.Nxa3 Qa5+ wins a piece for Black.

(794)
24.hxg6 wins one of Black's tripled isolated pawns, with the threat **25.Qh7#. 24...Nf6** is the best defense, but it allows **25.Bxe6+** and Black loses major material. The actual game continued **24...Rf6 25.Qh7+ Kf8 26.Qh8#.**

(795)
9...Nxf3+ is a clearance allowing **10.Bxf3 Qxf4.**

(796)
33.Rc6#

(797)
42.Nd4+ forks the King and the e-pawn that was about to Queen.

(798)
23...Ne2+ forks the White King and Queen.

(799)
11.c5 forks the Black Bishop and Knight.

(800)
30.Be4 pins the Black Rook to the King, allowing White to trade down to an easy endgame.

(801)
51.Qe8 pins and adds a second attacker to the Black Bishop on e7, and threatens the move **52.Rxe7+** winning a piece, and forking the Black King and Queen. If **51...Kf6 52.Bb4** skewering the Rook and adding an X-ray attacker to the Bishop on e7.

(802)
31...e4 attacks the pinned Bishop, **32.dxe4 dxe4** and Black will win the pinned piece.

(803)
18...Nxg4+ wins a pawn (the f-pawn is pinned), and the Knight now attacks the weak e3-pawn, which cannot be defended after the White King gets out of check.

(804)
20...d4 attacks the White Queen, and threatens mate with **21...Qg2#.** White cannot stop the mate.

(805)
27.Bxh6 Discovered attack on the Black Queen with the threat Qxg7#. Black will lose the Queen or be mated.

(806)
26.bxc6!! got a double exclam from Deep Rybka. This move removes the defender of the Black Bishop on d8, and discovers an attack on the Black Rook on b8. White is threatening a back rank mate, and wins a piece. Black cannot save the Rook and protect the Bishop.

(807)
24.Ra8+ Nb8 25.Bxb7#

(808)
29...Nxe4 takes a piece with a discovered attack on the Rook on b2. White cannot recapture and save the Rook at the same time.

(809)
39.b7 and the b-pawn cannot be stopped from queening.

(810)
27.Bxd4 wins a pawn, and pins the Black Bishop to the Black King, preventing Bxd6, *27...Bxd4 Qxd4* and White goes into an winning endgame.

(811)
20...Qh2+ 21.Kf1 Qh1#

(812)
9.Qxh7# A common mating pattern seen in scholastic games.

(813)
29...Qc1#

(814)
28.Qd8+ Qf8, the only way to get out of check. *29.Bxh7+!* Overloading the Black King like a New Delhi bus at rush hour, and winning a pawn. Black resigned. The game might have continued *29...Kf7 30.Bg6+* (another overload) *30...Kg8 31.Qh4* and Black will have to give up a lot of material to avoid mate.

(815)
15.Nxe6 sticks a fork in the Black Queen and Rook.

(816)
17.Bxh7+ Kxh7 18.Qh5 Kg8 19.Ne7# A nice combination of the 'Greek Gift' and Anastasia's mate patterns.

(817)
27.Bb3 forks the Black Rook and Queen.

(818)
51...Nc4+ forks the White King and Rook.

(819)
13.Ne5 adds a second attacker to the very weak f7-square, punishing Black for his unusual opening development.

(820)
23.Qxa6#

(821)
37.Rxf4 removes the defender of the Black Bishop on d4, *37...exf4 38.Rxd4* and White wins a Bishop and Knight for a Rook.

(822)
18.Rxf6 grabs an undefended piece. Moves like this, where both sides miss a piece that is just sitting there, are more common than you might imagine. This is especially true in scholastic games, and on correspondence sites, where both players might be playing a large number of games at the same time, and there might be days between moves.

(823)
27.f6+ forks the Black Knight and King.

(824)
8...Qh4 A textbook Fishing Pole attack. White cannot stop the checkmate. The game ended *9.Re1 Qxf2+ 10.Kh1 Qh4 11.Be3 Qxh2#.*

(825)
14...Bd4+ forks the White King and Queen.

(826)
21.Qc4+ sets up a 'Philidor's Legacy' smothered mate pattern, *21...Kh8 22.Nf7+ Kg8 23.Nh6+ Kh8 24.Qg8+ Rxg8 25.Nf7#.*

(827)
10.a5, cutting off the only escape-square for the Black Queen. White can trap the Queen on the next move with *11.Ra4.*

(828)
23...Bxb2 forks the White Rooks.

(829)
23...Ne3+ Family fork. The White Bishop on f2 is pinned.

(830)
45...Rh1 threatening 46...c1=Q, *46.Rxc2 Rh2+* skewers the White King and Rook.

(831)

In the diagram position Black played **18...Qxe3**, which seems logical. Black is up a piece, and can trade down into a winning endgame. Black eventually won 37 moves later. But a more brutal move would have been **18...Bc5** pinning the rook to the white king. Black can then take the rook (**19...Bxe3**) on his next move, and White cannot recapture, because the d-pawn protecting the White Rook on e3 is pinned to its Queen on d1, which could be captured by the Black Rook on d8. This leaves Black up an entire rook, and really destroys White's position. In a game where each person gets 21 days per move, this can save literally months, and possibly years, of effort.

If White does move his Queen to get out of the d-file pin, instead of getting the King out of the Bishop pin, then White can play **19...Rxd2**, and the White Rook on e3 is still pinned. Note that the Bishop moving to c5 created a nice Queen and Rook battery on the e-file as well.

When you see a good move, look for a better one – Emanuel Lasker.

(832)

23.Re6#

(833)

11...Rxg2 wins a pawn, and traps the White Queen.

(834)

34.Ne6+ forks the Black King and Queen.

(835)

9.Ba3+ and Black has to give up the Queen to get out of check.

(836)

Black sacrificed a Rook on h2 on the previous move to set up **31...Nf3+** (double discovered check) **32.Kh3 Rh8+ 33.Kg4 Nh2#**. A beautiful come from behind victory!

(837)

12.Ne5 threatens the weak doubled pawn on c6, and sets up a sneaky plan to trap the Black Bishop on g4 with h3, g4, f5, etc.

(838)

24.fxe6 wins a pawn and if **24...fxe6??** **25.Bxe6+** forks the Black King and Rook on c8.

(839)

26...Qd5 and mate on g2 cannot be stopped.

(840)

12.d4 attacks the Black Bishop on c5, and discovers an attack on the Black Queen on g5.

(841)

19...e4 forks the Queen and Knight.

(842)

9.dxe5 threatens the misplaced Black Bishop on d6, and clears the way for Qd5 threatening mate on f7. A sample line: **9...Nxe5 10.Nxe5 Bxe5 11.Qd5** forks the Rook on a8 and the f7-pawn.

(843)

32...Qh3 and mate with **33...Qg2#** next move.

(844)

23...Bd4+ 24.Ke1 Qxc1# wins the Queen with checkmate.

(845)

25.Rxe7!! deflects the Black Queen from protection of the Rook on b8, winning a critical pawn, and laying the groundwork for more tactical traps. If the Queen moves, White follows up with the killer **26.Nxe6+** and if **25...Qxe7 26.Qxb8 Qe8 27.Qxd6+** forking the Black King and Knight. Black can play **27...Qe7**, but then **28.Qxc5! Qxc5 29.Nxe6+** wins.

(846)

6...Qxg2 with a variation on the Blackburne Shilling Gambit. This move ignores the hanging Knight on e5, and takes the g2-pawn, threatening mate. Saving the Rook with **7.Rf1** leads to mate with **7...Qxe4+ 8.Qe2 Qxe2#**. This is a good opening trap to know.

(847)

34.Rxg6+ storming the barricades:
If **34...Qg7 35.Qxg7#**.
If **34...hxg6 35.Qxg6+ Qg7 36.Qxg7#**.
If **34...Kf7 35.Rg7+** skewers the Black King and Queen.

(848)

18...Qxd2 takes a piece that is defended once and attacked twice. Nothing tricky, but this was missed in the game, and Black played Qd3?? instead.

(849)
11.b4 attacks the pinned Knight.

(850)
54.Rxd5 wins a pawn, and if **54...Bxd5 55.Kxd5** trades down into an easily won endgame.

(851)
9.dxe5 attacks the Black Queen on f6, and discovers an attack on the Black Knight on b6. Black cannot save both at the same time.

(852)
33...Rxg5 gets Black out of check, and after **34.Bxg5** (or **34.Rxg5**) Black can play **34...Rd1+!!** with a discovered attack on the White Queen on c6 allowing **35...Qxc6**.

(853)
19...Qe3 and White cannot stop the mate threats of **Qf2#** and **Ng3#**.

(854)
11...b5 traps the White Bishop.

(855)
38...Re1# A back rank mate.

(856)
11.Nf5+ forks the Black King, the Bishop and the g7-pawn. Black cannot hold on to all of them. **11...Ke6 12.Nxg7+** and Black's best option is to give up the Rook with **12...Rxg7** as the King has no good squares.

(857)
17...Nxe2+ 18.Qxe2 Bxc3 19.Nxc3 Qd4+ forks the White Knight and King winning a piece.

(858)
18.Bxc6 removes one of the defenders of the e7-square in a position filled with deflections, overloads, forks and mate threats. Sample line: **18...Bxc6 19.Rxc6 f6 20.Qxf5 Qxf5 21.Nxe7+**.

(859)
33.Qg6+ is mate in 2: **33...Kh8 34.Nf7#** or **33...Kf8 34.Qf7#**.

(860)
45.Qd4 pins the Black Queen to the King. White will trade down into a won endgame.

(861)
18.Rxc5 The b-pawn is pinned. If **18...bxc5 19.Rxb7** winning two Bishops for the Rook.

(862)
13...Bg4 attacks the White Queen, which has no escape-squares. White can create an escape-square with **14.Bxh7+**, but has to give up a piece.

(863)
48.Qxf6 wins a pawn. The g7-pawn is pinned.

(864)
17.Rf7+ and Black has to give up the Queen with **17...Qe7** or get mated, **17...Ke8 18.Rh7+ Kf8 18.Qf7#**.

(865)
22.Nb5#

(866)
43.Rb8+! deflects the Black Rook from the defense of the Queen. **43...Rxb8 44.Qxa6**. If **43...Kh7 44.Qxa8** wins the Rook.

(867)
37.Rc1 pins the Black Queen to the King.

(868)
22...Qd2 and White cannot stop the mate threat **23.Rf1 Qxf2+ 24.Rxf2 Rc1 25.Rf1 Rxf1#**.

(869)
25.Re8+ Bf8 26.Qa8 adds a second attacker to the pinned Bishop on f8, which cannot be defended a second time. Note that playing **25.Qa8** first doesn't work because of **25...Rd8**.

(870)
40...Re2 paves the way for the d-pawn. If **41.Rxe2 dxe2** and the pawn can't be stopped. If **41.cxd3 Rxg2** and Black is up a Rook. If **41.Rg1 dxc2** and the Black Bishop covers the queening-square.

(871)
18.Nf4 traps the Black Queen. Black can get out of it with **18...Nxf2+** but gives up a Knight in the process.

(872)
24...Qg1+ 25.Kd2 Qxf2 26.Kc3 Rxe3+ 27.Kb4 c5 forks the White King and Queen.

(873)
24.Qxe5+ takes the hanging piece with check, and unleashes the battery of Rooks on the f-file.

(874)
52.Rg8# An Arabian Mate.

(875)
11.Bxe6 and Black is in more trouble than it might appear. If **11...dxe6 12.Bg5 Qd7** or any move on the d-file, **13.Rfd1** with a mate threat of **14.Rd8#**. Black will have to give up the Queen. Black's best option is to just give up the piece right away, and castle.

(876)
31...Bh2+ 32.g3 Re4# A mid field QB sac.

(877)
7...Nxf2 forks the Rook and Bishop.

(878)
30.Qxd7+ forces the Black King to the d-file where it can be pinned. **30...Kxd7 31.c3** attacking the pinned Bishop.

(879)
34...fxe6 captures the White Queen (just making sure you are paying attention!). Black will follow up with Nd5 and win the c3 pawn, with a winning endgame.

(880)
11.g3 traps the Black Queen.

(881)
18...Rxb2 allows **19 Qxb2 Nxd5** with a discovered attack on the White Queen. Black wins two pieces for the Rook.

(882)
23.Bxg7+ wins a pawn, and forks the Black King and Rook.

(883)
17...Qe1+ with the mate threat **18.Bf1 Bh3** and **19...Qxf1#**.

(884)
9.Nxe5 dxe5 10.Qc6+ forks the King and Bishop.

(885)
12.Qxg5+ picks up a loose pawn. **12...Kf8** is the best defense, when **13.Qxf4** grabs a second pawn.

(886)
23.Rb8+ leads to mate: **23...Kd7 24.Qb5+ Rc6 25.Qxc6#**.

(887)
13...Bg4 adds a second attacker and pins the White Knight on f3. If **14.Nf5 Rxf5 15.exf5 e4** attacking the pinned Knight.

(888)
23...Qg4#

(889)
15...Qh4+ Black comes crashing in. The g-pawn is pinned. **16.Kg1 Bxg3**

(890)
30...Nf4 attacks the White Queen with the Knight and the Rook, and threatens **31...Qxg2#**. If the Queen moves, there is a back rank mate threat as well.

(891)
8...Rg7 saves the Black Rook, attacking the White Queen. After the Queen retreats, Black can play **9...dxc3** winning the White Knight.

(892)
43...Rxf2+ 44.Kxf2 c2 and Black will Queen a pawn. **45.Rc6 b3 46.Ke3 b2 47.Rxc2 b1=Q**

(893)
26...Rb2#

(894)
24.Bd4+ forks the Black King and the dangerous c3-pawn, winning it before it can do any damage. **24...Kxe4 25.Bxc3**

(895)
14.Qc4+ forks the Black King and Bishop.

(896)
11.Qxg4 grabs the hanging piece at the end of a Bxf7 combo.

(897)
11...Bg4+ skewers the White King and Queen. If **12.Kd3** (or **12.Ke1** or **12.Ke3**) **12...Qg3+** If **12.Kf2 Qf6+**. If **12.Kd2 Qxd4+** followed by **13...Bxd1**.

(898)
14.f6 forks the Black Knight and Bishop.

(899)
13.Ne5+ forks the Black King and Bishop, which is now doubly attacked.

(900)
29.Bxb4 wins a piece – the c-pawn is pinned to the Black Queen by the White Rook.

(901)
44.Ne7+ forks the Black King and Rook.

(902)
34...b6 traps the White Bishop. If *35.Bd7* attacking the Black Rook *35...bxc5 36.Bxe6+ Kxe6* wins two Bishops for the Rook.

(903)
29...Kg6 The only way to get out of check that wins for Black. Blocking with *29...Be7* loses to *30.Rxf2* and *29...Kg8* loses to *30.Qe8+ Bf8 31.Qxe6 Kh8 32.Rxf2.*

(904)
28...Qa1# and White has too many irons in the fire.

(905)
16...Nxd2 and White doesn't have time to recapture and guard against the threat of *17...Be4* pinning the White Queen to the King.

(906)
20...Bxh2+ and all of Black's pieces are ready to spring into action. After *21.Kh1* (*21.Kf2 Qg3#*), Black activates his Rook with *21...Rh4* setting up a discovered check with ideas like *22...Be5+* and can also bring in additional attackers with moves like *22...Ng4,* depending on White's response. Black has too many attackers, and White has too few defenders to survive this attack.

(907)
40...Bd4+ and White has to give up the exchange or lose the Queen: *41.Rf2 Bxf2 42.Kxf2 Qxf1+ 43.Kxf1* and Black has an easily won endgame.

(908)
43...Ra1 forcing a trade of Rooks into an easily won endgame. Finding moves like this can save you a lot of time and energy in grueling weekend tournaments.

(909)
23.Qh6 Rg8 Black stops the mate on g7, but can't stop the mate on h7: *24.Rf3 g5 25.Rh3 Rac8 26.Qxh7#.*

(910)
27.Nxh6 takes a piece that is attacked twice and defended only once.

(911)
30...Qe1+ 31.Rxe1 fxe1=R# or *31...fxe1=Q#.*

(912)
22.Ba7+ Ka8 23.Rc8+ Bb8 24.Rxb8#

(913)
12.Nd6+!! and Black has to give up his Queen to avoid mate: *12...Bxd6 13.Bxd8* or *12...Kf8 13.Qxf7#.*

(914)
29...Rg1+! 30.Kxg1 (or *30.Kh2*) *30...Nf3+* forking the King and Queen.

(915)
17...Qc5+ On the previous move White played f4 to 'kick the Queen', but this backfired, creating this forking opportunity of King and Bishop.

(916)
22.Rh3+ Kg8 24.Ne7# Anastasia's mate.

(917)
19.Bxd5+ forks the Black King and Bishop *19...Bxd6 20.Qxd5* (forking the King and Rook) *20...Nf7* (connecting the Rooks to get out of check) *21.Nxf7* wins a piece. If *21...Rxf7 22.Qxa1+.*

(918)
40.Rxg6!! clears the way to protect his passed pawn on g7. If *40...Qxg6 41.Rg3* Black Queen moves, then White Queens a pawn with *42.g8=Q+.* This was a clever way for White to protect his passed pawn.

(919)
21...Nd4 saves the Black Knight, which was under attack, and adds a third attacker to the Knight on f3 which is 'threat pinned' because of the checkmate ...Qh1#. *22.Bxd4 cxd4* and White cannot save the Knight on c3 which is attacked by the d4-pawn, and the Knight on f3 which is attacked twice, and defended only once.

(920)
38...Re1+ 39.Rxe1 Rxe1#

(921)
30.Rxg7+ overloads the Black King: *30...Kxg7 31.Qxe6.*

(922)
43.Be1# Black went a little too far using his King as an offensive weapon.

(923)
32...Ne2+!! forks the White King and Queen, and threatens a back rank mate with Rxd1.

(924)
49...Ne3+!! The crowning sacrifice which forks the White King and Knight, and will allow the b-pawn to Queen.

(925)
17.Nxg5+ wins a pawn breaking down Black's wall of pawn protection, and adds another attacker. If *17...hxg5 18.Qh5+ Kg8 19.Qxg6#.*

(926)
27...Qxf3!! and the double Bishop mate can't be stopped. *28.Re8+Kh7 29.Rh8+ Kxh8 30.gxf3 Bxf3#*

(927)
35.e7+ Discovered check, and White will Queen a pawn on the next move.

(928)
36...Ra1 pinning the White Rook to the White King. If *37.Rxa1 bxa1=Q.* The White Queen cannot protect the Rook and the Knight on c5 at the same time.

(929)
10.Bxe7 grabs a pawn with a discovered attack on the Black Queen by the White Rook on a1.

(930)
26.Be4 skewers the Black Queen and Rook.

(931)
29.Rxd7 wins a piece, deflecting the Black Queen. If *29...Qxd7 30.f7+* discovered check. Black cannot stop mate.

(932)
11.Nxe7 Qxe7 12.Bb4 skewers the Black Queen and Rook.

(933)
14.Rd1 pins and adds a second attacker to the Black Bishop on d4. *14...c5 15.c3* wins the Bishop.

(934)
33.Qa8+ and after the King moves, *34.c8=Q.*

(935)
15.Bg5 skewers the Black Queen and Rook. If *15...Qf5 16.Bd3* traps the Queen. Black can counterattack with *15...Nc3* but this still loses after *16.Bxf6 Nxd1 17.Bxd8* and Black is down a piece.

(936)
21...Qxh3+ 22.Kg1 Qg2#

(937)
45...Be5 forks the White Rook and Knight.

(938)
13.Qf7# White missed this move, and played *13.Qe6+*, then missed a second mate in one after *13...Be7* with *14.Bc4* instead of *14.Qf7#.*

(939)
10.Nf6+ A crushing double discovered check. *10...Kd8 11.Re8#.*

(940)
28.Be6#

(941)
11...Bg5 pins the White Queen to the King.

(942)
37...R8a3+ If *38.Kf4 Rf3#*, otherwise White has to give up the Knight with *38.Nc3* to prevent the immediate mate.

(943)
13.Bg5+ Bf6 14.Bxf6# A nice checkmate with the two Bishops.

(944)
17.gxh4 grabs the hanging Rook.

(945)
47...Ne3+ forks the White King and Rook.

(946)
13.Bxg8 Rxg8 14.Nxf6+ Kf7 15.Nxg4 wins a piece. Winning the Bishop on g4 is better than winning the exchange with 15.Nxg8.

(947)
12...Nxe2+ overloads the White Queen, who can't recapture and defend the White Knight on g5: *13.Qxe2 Qxg5.*

(948)
31.Re8+ Kd7 32.Rd8# or *31...Kb7 32.Rb8#*, both hook mates.

(949)
48...Re7+ deflects the White King from the protection of the White Bishop on f2: *49.Kd2 Bxf2* and White cannot stop the pawn from queening.

(950)
46.Qf6+ Kf8 47.Rh8# (or *47.Qh8#*)

(951)
8...Qxa4 removes the defender of the c2-pawn. *9.Nxa4 Nc2+* forks the White King and Rook.

(952)
14...Qf3 threatens mate on e2: *15.Kf1 Bxh3+ 16.Ke1* (*16.Rxh3 Qxf2#*) *16...Bg4 17.Kf1 Qxh1#.*

(953)
6.dxe5 attacks the pinned Knight on f6. *6...h6 7.Bh4 g5 8.exf6 gxh4 9.exd5* (attacking the second pinned Knight) *Qxf6 10.dxc6* and White is up a piece, and Black's pawn structure is in bad shape. In the game White played Nxe5, which wins a pawn, but misses a bigger opportunity.

(954)
21...Ng3+ forks the White King and Rook. *22.Kh2 Nxf1+*

(955)
51.b6 and the pawn cannot be stopped.

(956)
6.Bb5+ A discovered attack on the Black Queen. *6...c6 7.Qxd4 1-0*

(957)
7...Nxf3+ is a Zwischenzug. Both White and Black have pieces under attack. Black trades off his attacked piece with check, then will play *8...Bxb5* on the next move, winning a piece.

(958)
29...Rh1+!! 30.Kxh1 Nf2+ forks the King and Queen leaving Black up a piece.

(959)
41.Rb6!! is a nice tactic that accomplishes multiple things at one time. It attacks the Black Rook on b5, it threatens *42.Bf3#*, and the Rook move protects the White Bishop on b7, which was hanging. It is pretty because the Rook can be captured in two different ways by both the Rook and Bishop, and also ignores the Bishop that is hanging.

(960)
23...Nh3# Smothered mate. The g-pawn is pinned, and White's two Knights are as useless as a chocolate teapot.

(961)
15...Ng4 unleashes a discovered attack on the White Bishop on g5, and a triple attack on the vulnerable f2-pawn, which is only defended twice.

(962)
28...Rxc3!! wins a pawn that appears to be defended. If *29.Qxc3 Nf3+* with a discovered double attack. *30.Kf1 Qxc3.*

(963)
12...Qd5 forks the White Knight and Rook.

(964)
12...Nxd4 grabs a pawn that appears safe. If *13.Qxd4 Ne4* with a discovered X-ray attack on the White Queen and Knight.

(965)
38...Rd3+ forks the White King and Knight.

(966)
32...Nxa4 An X-ray tactic winning a Rook.

(967)
11...Nxc2+ Family Fork.

(968)
22...Qxc1!! wins a Rook. White can't recapture because of the back rank mate threat. **23.Rxc1 Re1+ 24.Rxe1 Rxe1#**

(969)
52...Nd6+ forces White to trade off his last remaining piece.

(970)
23...Qxf1+ 24.Kxf1 Re1#

(971)
30...Qc6 forces a trade of Queens into a easily won endgame.

(972)
5...Qxd1+ 6.Kxd1 Bxb5 wins a piece. In the game Black went for **5...Qxg2** which only wins a pawn after **6.Bxd7 Nxd7 7.Qf3**.

(973)
24...d4+ 25.Bf3 Bxf3+ 26.Qxf3 Qxf3+ and Black trades into an easily won endgame.

(974)
9...Bxd3 removing the defender of the c2-pawn. **10.cxd3 Nc2+ 11.Kf1 Nxa1**

(975)
17.Qg7#

(976)
18...f4 traps the White Bishop.

(977)
26.Rc5 pins the Black Queen to the King.

(978)
47.Rd6+ forks the Black King and Bishop.

(979)
21.Rc8+ Rxc8 22.Rxc8+ Ka7 23.Qb8#

(980)
29...Nd2# A crazy end to a crazy game where both sides went on King hunts.

(981)
18...Nxg5 wins a piece that is only defended once and attacked twice.

(982)
5.dxe5 Bxe5 6.f4 Bd6 7.e5 forks the Black Knight and Bishop.

(983)
23...Qxf2+ 24.Kh1 Qh1+! 25.Rxf1 Rxf1#

(984)
36...Re2 leads to mate. If **37.Rc2 Nf5** (threatening a double Knight mate) **38.Rg1 Rd1** (pinning, deflecting and threatening **39...Rxg1#**) **39.Rxd1 Ng3#**, if **37.Rxf3 Nxf3 38.Any Rh2#**. Arabian Mate.

(985)
59.Kf3 gets the opposition on the Black King. All other moves draw. The game might continue **59...Kh4 60.Kf4 b5 61.axb5 axb5 62.Kf5 Kg3 63.g5 hxg5** followed by a racc to the Queenside, which White will win. White grabs the b4-pawn, and will promote to a Queen.

(986)
11...Nxd3+ sets up **12.Qxd3 Qa5+** forking the White King and the Knight on f5, winning a piece. **13.Kf1 Qxf5**

(987)
24...Bd5 adds a second and third attacker to the Knight at the same time. The White Knight is pinned to the White Queen, and a third defender cannot be added, so the piece will be lost.

(988)
41.f5 forks the Black Queen and Knight.

(989)
15.Nxe5! grabs a pawn that appears to be protected, but really isn't. The Black Knight on g6 is pinned by the White Queen to the Black King, and the f6-pawn is pinned by the White Bishop to the Black Queen.

(990)
19.Qe5+ Be6 20.Qxe6# A forced mate in two that was missed in the game. The f6-pawn is pinned.

(991)
24...Qxg2# The Queen and Knight work well together for checkmate.

(992)
24.Rxe4 wins a piece. If **24...fxe4 25.Bxe4** forks the Black King and the Rook on a8.

(993)
21.Nd5+ Ke6 22.Ng5# is a nice mate with the two Knights.

(994)
22...Qh7# A long distance checkmate that was missed in the game.

(995)
8...f3#

(996)
15...Bxe2 In this position both sides have pieces hanging, so move order is important. **15...Bxe2**

is best because it attacks the White Queen. After **16.Qxe2 Kxg7** Black comes out ahead a piece.

(997)
22.Bxf6 removing the defender from the h7 mating-square. Black does not have time to recapture and defend against **23.Qh7#** and will lose material.

(998)
45...Rg3+!! got a double exclam from Fritz 13. **46.fxg3 Rf1#** slays the Dragon.

(999)
37...f5+ with a discovered attack on the unprotected White Rook on h7. **38.Kxf5 Rxh7**

(1000)
24.Qxd5! wins a piece. If **24...Qxd5 25.Ne7+** forking the Black King and Queen.

(1001)
38.Qh8+ Kg5 39.Qh4# (or **39.h4#**)

Final Thoughts

Questions Or Comments?

We would love to hear your thoughts. If any of the problems were confusing we would be happy to help explain the answer. Email Tim at tim@tacticstime.com and Anthea at nth_carson@yahoo.com.

Acknowledgements

I could not have done a project like this without all of the people who take the time to enter their games into the computer, post their games on the internet, and have sent me their game collections to use.
These include:

Paul Anderson	Richard 'Buck' Buchanan	Jeff Baffo
Pete Short	Joel Johnson	Johnny Mac
Francisco Baltier	Andy Pineda	Kenzie Moore
Fred Spell	Bob Crume	Edson Cortiano
Jerry Maier	Robert Rountree	Tomasz Pintel
Bill Chandler	Carl Hamre	William Parker
Anthea Carson	Ed Stoddard	Aravind Suresh
Shannon Fox	William Parker	Priyav Chandna
Dean Brown	Eric King	Randy Reynolds
Chris Peterson	Geoff Chandler	Tim Tran
Brian Wall	Rob Hartelt	Aaron Pauls

Many other people sent me games as well, and I am very thankful!
Entering games by hand from score sheets into a PGN format can be a painful job, and I am fortunate that there are a lot of people who spent hours doing this.
Thank you to readers who helped me edit, and catch errors, and provided good ideas and feedback, including:

Joey Guitian	Chris Kim	Graham Diggins
Peter Horecky	Edson Cortiano	Andy Smith
Fred Jarmuz	Jon Wooldridge	William Parker
Art Cunningham	José de Anchieta	Tijs Van Oevelen
Joel Johnson	Jeff Davis	Barak Yedidia
Geoff Chandler	Rodolfo Pardi	Joel Lecorre
Stephen Dann	Hank Anzis	Richard Sloanaker

I am also grateful to the following websites that helped to provide me with raw game scores:
http://www.coloradochess.com
http://www.renochess.org
http://www.redhotpawn.com
http://www.nwchess.com
http://www.metrowestchess.org
http://games.groups.yahoo.com/group/UnorthodoxChessOpenings/
http://wyomingchess.com/

http://www.taom.com/pipermail/brianwall-chesslist/
http://cschess.webs.com/
http://eagleandking.webs.com/
http://www.angelfire.com/co/cscc/
http://www.chessclub.com
http://www.timmybx.com
http://www.denverchess.com
http://columbiachess.com/
http://kansaschess.org
http://georgiachess.org
http://www.scchess.org/
http://www.pscfchess.org
http://www.sdchess.org/
http://www.lincolnchessfoundation.org
http://nsca.nechess.com/
http://www.burlingamechessclub.com
http://www.westmichiganchess.com
http://ficsgames.com/
http://www.reddit.com/r/chess/
http://www.chess.com

Don't Forget

To get more fun chess tactics from real player games, along with tips and tricks to help improve your chess game, click the link below to subscribe to the award winning 'Tactics Time Chess Improvement E-Mail Newsletter'...
http://tacticstime.com/newsletter

Unfortunately, life is not like a book of tactics exercises...

Nobody will tap you on your shoulder when the position you are looking at contains a tactical blow. However, Emmanuel Neiman offers help. He improves your tactics antenna: you will learn to read the 7 main signals that indicate you must start looking for a win.

With lots of examples and exercises.

paperback ♦ 240 pages ♦ €24.95 / $28.95 ♦ available at your local (chess)bookseller or at newinchess.com ♦ a NEW IN CHESS publication

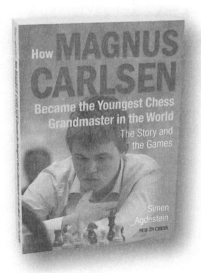

The fairy-tale-like story of Magnus Carlsen's rise

"From beginners' errors to better and better achievements, the reader learns how a real chess prodigy develops, temporary setbacks and disappointments included ... One has to give great praise to the author for his honesty and empathy and for the unselfish way he tells the story."
Heinz Brunthaler, Rochade Europa Magazine

paperback ♦ 192 pages ♦ €19.95 / $19.95 ♦ available at your local (chess)bookseller or at newinchess.com ♦ a NEW IN CHESS publication

Vital Lessons for Every Chess Player

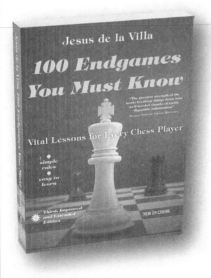

"If you really have no patience for endgames, at least read Jesus de la Villa's '100 Endgames You Must Know'." – *Gary Walters Chess*

"The greatest strength of the book: breaking things down into well-worded chunks of easily digestible information." – *Marsh Towers Chess Reviews*

"De la Villa does the job quite well. He emphasizes the practical and prefers understanding to memorization." – *IM John Donaldson, jeremysilman.com*

paperback ♦ 256 pages ♦ €21.95 / $24.95 ♦ available at your local (chess)bookseller or at newinchess.com ♦ a NEW IN CHESS publication

Not just another collection of interesting positions

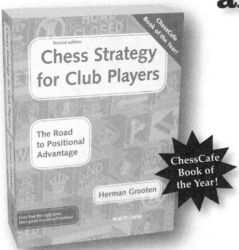

"One of my three favorite chess teaching books. Grooten supplies nice examples and great explanation in a very structured way." – *Jan van de Mortel, Chess Education Partners*

"A fantastic and challenging book for ambitious and advanced club players." – *KARL Magazine*

"Chess coaches will have a quality supply of superb examples and explanations, and self-motivated students will benefit immensely if they are over, say, 1800 in strength." – *Pete Tamburro, ChessLife*

paperback ♦ 400 pages ♦ €25.95 / $29.95 ♦ available at your local (chess)bookseller or at newinchess.com ♦ a NEW IN CHESS publication